African Christian Spirituality

African Christian
Spirituality

Edited with an Introduction by
Aylward Shorter W.F.

Geoffrey Chapman
London

A Geoffrey Chapman book published by
Cassell Ltd.
35 Red Lion Square, London WC1R 4SG
and at Sydney, Auckland, Toronto and Johannesburg
an affiliate of
Macmillan Publishing Co. Inc.
New York

ISBN 0 225 66238 8

Printed in Great Britain by
Fletcher & Son Ltd, Norwich

*This book belongs
to the whole of Africa,
but in the first place
to Uganda,
home of martyrs,
in gratitude
for eight memorable years.
(1968-1975)*

Contents

Foreword

'African Christian Spirituality' is the name given to this collection of extracts from the spiritual writings of Africans.
All twenty writers represented are Africans, and they come
from ten English and French-speaking African countries in
East, West, Central and Southern Africa. Some of the writers
are statesmen whose names are household words, and some
are lesser known politicians. Many are bishops, priests, pas-
tors and members of religious orders, and some are laymen
and laywomen. A few are well known as writers already, but
the majority are probably unknown to the general reading
public. Nearly all are professing Christians, though one or
two would not describe themselves as such. All, however,
would probably admit to being strongly influenced by
Christianity. Three writers, Kaunda, Kayoya and Omoyajowo, describe their philosophy of life as 'humanism', but
all represent the simultaneous recovery of human values by
Africa and by the Christian Church.

Making an anthology is always a somewhat personal exercise. Readers and critics will, no doubt, immediately think of
other authors and other passages that should have been
included in such a collection as this. This collection of
prose and poetry certainly represents the editor's personal
tastes and range of contacts. It is also strongly influenced by
his association for ten years with the *African Ecclesiastical
Review* and *Gaba Publications*. Grateful acknowledgement
of permissions granted by authors, editors and publishers is
made at the end of this book. The collection is not intended
to be exhaustive. One would rather hope that it could be the

first of many spiritual anthologies from Africa.

This book was originally the idea of Sarah Baird-Smith. Thanks are due to her in the first place, and afterwards to her successor at Geoffrey Chapman Publishers, John Stockdale, who was equally enthusiastic about the project. Thanks are also due to Mr. Hugo Kamya of Uganda who helped in the selection and copying of the texts. Perhaps a final word should also be said about the role of the editor of this anthology. The goal of a missionary in Africa is to give way to African Christians, allowing them to speak for themselves and to take the evangelization of the African continent into their own hands. This is part — an important part — of the social revolution for which the missionary is working. As President Julius Nyerere of Tanzania has said, social revolutions are usually led by those who were beneficiaries under the system they are trying to replace. A missionary, therefore, need make no apology for identifying himself with the revolution demanded by these African Christian writers. Another missionary task is to be a 'link-person'. Camillus Lyimo supports the editor's contention that African writers and thinkers are not influencing one another sufficiently. A book like this is one way of bringing them together. It is also a means of communicating the thought of African Christian writers to readers outside Africa. As such, it helps to realize the new image of the universal Church — a fellowship of local churches, exchanging their Christian vision with one another, acting and reacting in turn.

Aylward Shorter W.F.
Dar-es-Salaam, Tanzania
September 1977

Part One
African Christian Spirituality

1 Spiritual Writing in Contemporary Africa

The last two decades have witnessed the birth of a new liter-
ary tradition in Africa.[1] The arts of story-telling, recitation,
dance, mime and the dramatic representations of spirit-
mediums, which were all part of the oral literature of
ancient Africa, have flowered in the written works of modern Africans, expressing themselves for the most part in English and French. One after another, novelists, poets,
playwrights, philosophers and historians have tried to inter-
pret the experience of their peoples, the trauma of colonization, the hopes and ideals engendered by political
independence, the hard-won triumphs and also the harsh
realities of life in contemporary Africa. Unpopular though
this prophetical role often is, it has made its impact through
university departments, school literature syllabuses, libraries and travelling theatre.

African writers certainly do not neglect their people's religious experience, for religion in Africa is a phenomenon
that cannot be ignored — a mountain which, like a Kenya or
a Kilimanjaro, is part of the African landscape. Faithfully
they portray the anguish and misunderstanding that
attended the encounter of Christianity with traditional religion, the birth of religious movements of protest in colonial
times and — with a wistful nostalgia — the simplicity and
mystery of rural religious practice. Yet it cannot be said that
the majority of African writers are sympathetic towards the
new religion or indeed that they show any profound understanding of it. Many are frankly hostile. As a result, it has certainly escaped general notice that in this jostling crowd

there is a handful of highlanders who are really at home
among the peaks — a few who fully possess the Christian
message, who are able to integrate it with their African religious tradition and who see its relevance in a developing
continent. Some are well-known statesmen who, perhaps,
do not often 'let their religion show'. A very few are celebrated writers. But the majority are church leaders and
church people whose writings are dispersed and relatively
unrecognized. This book is an attempt to draw the threads
together and to see what pattern emerges.

It must not be thought that this spiritual pattern has yet
been imposed on the mass of African Christians, or that
these ideas have yet percolated down to every level in the
churches. Efforts are certainly being made in that direction,
notably through religious education syllabuses based on
life experience, but it is still too early to judge the effect of
these new syllabuses on the outlook of African Christians.[2]
An important plank in the platform of these spiritual writers (for that is what they must be called) is that much of popular Christianity in modern Africa is extremely shallow,
that it is a form of excapism bred by underdevelopment — a
'religiosity', as Kayoya calls it, and nothing more.[3] These
writers are spiritual writers because they advocate an authentic spirituality, a living religion or religion in action.

The word 'spirituality' is Christian in origin. Like many
other words in the Christian vocabulary it has been deval-
ued to the level of 'anaemia' and banality, and denotes a religion characterized by an interior or inward emphasis. This
is precisely what spirituality, in the mouths of early Christians and of modern African Christian writers, is not meant
to be. Spirituality is a dynamic and outgoing concept. The
very word derives from *spiritus*, the lifegiving force which
stems from God, quickens the baptized Christian and transforms the relationships he has with his fellow human
beings. There is nothing cerebral or esoteric about spirituality; it is the core of the Christian experience, the encounter
with God in real life and action. Spirituality is the same
thing as continuous or experiential prayer — prayer as a living communion with God who is experienced as being personally present in the relationships of humanity. It is the
mode of living, the essential disposition, of the believer, and

it imparts a new dimension to the believer's life. In other words, it is not only a new way of looking at human life, but a new way of living it. It is unnecessary, perhaps, to draw any sharp dividing line between theology and spirituality. Theology should be spiritual theology. That is to say, it should not be merely speculative, but should encourage active commitment.

It follows that, by extension, the concept of spirituality can be applied to every religious system, and that the traditional religions of Africa can be said to have a spirituality. Of course, one cannot begin to speak of the spirituality of religious traditions in Africa without confronting the methodological problems involved in the study of these religions.[4] The comparative analysis of African religions is still in its infancy, and even if it were far advanced, it probably would not allow us to draw conclusions which were of equal validity for all the traditions. Serious studies favour the historical and categorical approaches which reveal African Traditional Religion as an essentially plural phenomenon. In spite of this fact, the reaction of African spiritual writers to traditional religious diversity is, in many ways, a unified reaction. It has been said, for example, that all modern African writers are 'romantic anthropologists', and this is certainly true of the spiritual writers. Romanticizing is not necessarily unhealthy, as long as one keeps one's critical faculty alive also. In the last hundred years or so an enlargement, too, of the theological horizon has taken place in Africa. Numerous writers, speaking from a newly acquired Christian standpoint, have borrowed ideas and images from the religions of widely differing, African ethnic groups and have created a larger-than-life African religious philosophy. This is part of a conscious movement on the part of the African intelligentsia to return to their roots and to create a neo-African culture, and it is one of the great priorities of contemporary Africa. Few of these scholars are perhaps aware of the methodological assumptions that underlie their work, and much of the African religious genius, its vitality and originality, is necessarily sacrificed in the process. At a more general level, historical interaction and the movement of ideas have been such in traditional Africa that certain themes can be predicated of African Traditional Religion as a whole. Such themes are: the desire for abundant life, the emphasis on communitarian living, the effective memory of past events, the vital relationship between living and dead and the preoccupation with the human cause of evil. These and many other themes have been taken up by our spiritual writers and provide a partial explanation for the remarkable unanimity which characterizes their work.

African spiritual writers exhibit a striking consensus. We have just mentioned the common cultural foundation on which their work rests. There are many other factors which favour this consensus. The most important influences have been those stemming from new political philosophies and from a new theology, all of which place great emphasis on the human person, on human relationships and on human values. In the political sphere this humanism accompanied and followed the achievement of political independence in Africa. It has flowered in numerous ideologies, the most recognizably Christian of which are associated with the names of statemen such as Kaunda of Zambia, Senghor of Senegal and Nyerere of Tanzania. In the religious sphere this humanism accompanied the humanism of the Second Vatican Council and of the World Council of Churches' Assemblies at Uppsala and Nairobi, a Christian rediscovery of human values and a new theological emphasis on human cultures and development. Both the political and the theological lines of thought converge in the demand for co-operative living, for giving new dynamism to the ancient village world of Africa and for the building of authentic, human communities. Villagization goes hand in hand with Christian community building.[5]

There is no doubt that the thought of Karl Marx has made, and is making, an impact on contemporary Africa. In these spiritual writers the name of Marx provokes a universal reaction. In so far as he advocates an inhuman struggle or the use of 'depersonalizing' force, his doctrine is unwelcome. In so far as an atheistic faith is essential to its philosophy, Marxism is a poison to be strenuously rejected. On the other hand, there is another name which is frequently on the lips of these spiritual writers, one that is pronounced with admiration and respect. It is the name of the Jesuit anthropologist, theologian and poet, Teilhard de Chardin.

The evolutionary optimism, scientific rigour and all-embracing humanism of Teilhard have caught the African imagination, and it is from Teilhard that the hope springs for a technology without materialism and a development without depersonalization.

Undoubtedly, another factor in the African spiritual consensus is the common experience of human poverty and need, and the yearning for liberation and complete autonomy. There are still African countries ruled by white minority regimes, denying the African majority the dignity, security and fulfilment that belongs to every member of the human race. Such regimes are founded on violence and disdain. Even more disquieting and insidious is the violence and exploitation by those who use force to take power in independent African countries and who use that power for ends that are individually or collectively selfish. But the African experience of human degradation is part of a larger 'Third World' experience and that is why concepts like those of Liberation Theology, Black Consciousness and Black Theology have made such an impact on African spiritual writers. In their origin, these ideas come from the United States and South America, but they have been taken up with considerable vigour, particularly in South Africa. They are not so much a response to stimuli from another continent as an original re-application to the African situation of South American and Black concepts.

African spirituality is a Christian humanism, but it is essentially revolutionary. It is a four-fold revolt. Firstly, it is the revolt against materialism on the one hand and against a shallow religiosity on the other. Secondly, it is a revolt against a world that conspires to dehumanize, a 'white' world in which the structures are vitiated through their injustice to the black man. It is even a revolt against the unfair structures of a 'white' church. Thirdly it is a revolt against cultural passivity, against being a mere consumer of the products of western civilization. It is a call to a new creativity that has its roots in the African past. Finally, it is a revolt against a purely internal religion, a religion that is inward looking and oblivious of the community.

These four 'revolts' can also be expressed positively as commitments: the commitment to a world of the spirit, to

man and his integral development to culture as a living tradition and to human community. We shall introduce the
selection of texts that illustrate African Christian Humanism in this book under these headings.

2 A World of the Spirit

The unearthing of one's roots is an important aspect of establishing Black identity and African identity. That is why many African writers take the village world of rural Africa as their starting-point. It is there that they are closest to their own cultural tradition, to nature and, in most cases, to their own childhood memories. The commitment to culture is a question that must be treated on its own, but closeness to nature and the mystery and enchantment of childhood are closely related to the present theme, the apprehension of a world of the spirit. For Camara Laye life in the African countryside is a romance, but a romance of real life.[6] This kind of life is more intense, more singleminded than the life of technologically advanced towns and cities. It is, in a word, more 'civilized', since technology has little or nothing to do with civilization. It enables human beings to live at a greater depth and it gives free scope for the life of the soul. For Kenneth Kaunda it is not so much a question of romanticism as realism.[7] The rural-dwelling African lives a life of hardship as well as simplicity and this makes him humble. He inhabits a larger world than the townsman and he is therefore forced to ask big questions, even if his answers to these questions are crude and unsophisticated. The rural dweller is open to the spiritual dimension of life because he is less attached to, and less dependent on, material things.

Two ideas developed by anthropologists are useful in this connection. One is Victor Turner's concept of liminality and the other is Joseph Goetz' concept of cosmobiology.[8]

African rural life is a 'liminal' situation comparable to the threshold period in a rite of passage, when an initiant is passing from one state of life to another. In this unstructured state of freedom, silence and dispossession, when all social relationships, obligations and privileges are suspended and when all individuating differences are minimized, the initiant sees the world with a new pair of eyes. He experiences a new understanding of life and of human society. Rural life in Africa has a liminal quality which gives those who live it a deeper perception and which helps them to glimpse the world of the spirit. Cosmobiology is a name given to an understanding of the place of humanity in nature, which links the lifecycles of human beings with the rhythms that govern the whole universe, the days and nights, the movement of heavenly bodies, the seasons, the rotation of crops and the migrations of birds and animals. Human life reflects and extends these cosmic cycles. Perhaps a great measure of Teilhard de Chardin's appeal for writers like Kaunda, Senghor and Nyerere is explained by cosmobiological thinking in traditional Africa, for he also draws a continuum between humanity and the material world.

Closeness to nature also explains why Africans are generally at home in the Jewish Old Testament. A number of Black theologians and African theologians have published studies comparing African spirituality with that of the Old Testament, but it would seem that the similarities they adduce are based on characteristics shared by preliterate, rural societies all over the world.[9] Closeness to nature is generally accompanied by a belief in divine power at work even in secondary causes, a love of concrete imagery and symbolism, a reliance on oral traditions, an emphasis on the transmission of life, on personal relationships, on family, on hospitality and group loyalties. Of course, every human tradition has its own particular genius and there are also important differences between the African and Biblical traditions. One of these is the vital relationship between living and dead in Africa which finds no echo among the ancient Israelites, whose notions of an after-life were slow to develop. On the other hand, there is hardly a parallel in Africa for the detailed theological interpretation of Israel's

political history and her sense of a historical mission to the
nations. However, the point must be taken that similarities
exist, and that, if this is the case, it is not due, as some wild
speculators would have us believe, to a primitive revelation
or the wandering of a lost tribe of Israel, but to basic resem-
blances in the ways of life of rural peoples. Harold Turner
has classified a great many of the so-called African Independent Churches which are common today as 'Hebraist',
because they successfully adapt aspects of Old Testament
belief and practice to African religious tradition.[10] African
spiritual writers, however, do not make the mistake of
remaining in the Old Testament, but they understand the
relevance of rural life to a faith that is passionate and powerful.

The enchanted time of childhood is also invoked by spiritual writers engaged in the process of 'unearthing their
roots'. Kaunda, Laye and Kayoya all return to their childhood in their writing.[11] Childhood is not only a time of
humility and innocence. It is a time of mystery, of faith and
of prayers that are filled with trust. Childhood is also a condition of power, for childhood convictions and childhood
loves are unbreakably strong. The radiant King described by
Camara Laye, unquestionably an image of God himself,
turns out to be a slender adolescent whose adorable fragility
captivates the dying hero of his book.[12] In this appeal to
childhood the modern spiritual writer is returning to one of
the classic themes of African oral tradition, the power of the
weak. African oral literature is filled with myths and folk
tales that recount the miraculous exploits of a 'wonder-
child', a child that speaks from its mother's womb or immediately after birth, a child that puts its own parents to
shame, a child that saves people from the clutches of the
ogre that lives in the forest and so forth. Childhood thus
becomes the most eloquent symbol of the divine power at
work, rendered more visible and more striking when it is
manifested through what is ordinarily weak and insignifi-
cant. The symbol and the theme are, of course, well known
to Christianity also, and this fact is not missed by African
Christian writers.

Memories of childhood lead the spiritual writer in Africa
towards the concept of a spiritual universe, in which all

created things have a symbolic quality and everything
speaks, as Camara Laye puts it, of 'the mystery of the union
between heaven and earth'. The African soul cries out for
prodigies, refuses to believe that life consists merely in what
can be seen at a glance. The human being realizes that he is
not alone in the world. Air, earth, water, savannah, forest,
mountain are 'truly inhabited by genii', as Laye calls them,
and these, in the opinion of Harry Sawyerr, are human
attempts 'to establish concrete manifestations of the deity'.[13]

Kaunda, Kayoya, Laye all speak of the soul, but they give
slightly different emphases to this concept. Kayoya sees the
soul as the faculty which, in human beings, enables them to
appreciate values that go beyond themselves. Kaunda
speaks of the intuition of 'the unknowable' as an activity of
the soul, while Laye describes the soul's activity as the recognition that the inexplicable is supreme.[14] For Laye the
human soul is characterized by a strong desire for freedom
and by the ability to appreciate beauty, particularly in art.
The 'spiritless soul' is the soul which has been dulled and
deadened by the mechanical aids of technological life. The
soul has needs and these needs must be met. The soul, thinks
Kaunda, is the spiritual dimension that is integral to the
human personality. It is, above all, community-orientated,
the centre of a network of personal relationships. It is interesting that these writers do not speak of the soul in terms of
'life-force', 'power', 'vital force', etc. This confirms the
recent critique by Alexis Kagame of Placide Tempels' classic definition of 'being', according to Bantu Philosophy, as
force vitale.[15] Kagame has shown that in no Bantu language
is the idea of being or soul expressed as 'force'. The desire is
for life, a forceful life, a life that is full and abundant. Personality, life, existence are logically prior to power, force,
energy. Vital force is not a principle of being but a fulfilment of being. African spiritual writers echo this view
when, like Nyerere, and Lwasa, they quote the words of
Christ: 'I am come that they may have life and have it more
adundantly.''[16]

A spiritual view of human life in the world necessarily
entails a confrontation with death. Whereas in the western
world there is an elaborate conspiracy of silence about death
and everything is done to put it out of sight and mind, in

Africa — particularly in the rural areas — death is a stark reality with which everyone is familiar. Although death is a mystery, although it does violence to the weary man who clings to life, and although it is described in terms of 'silence' and 'immobility', it is nevertheless somehow a new beginning. In the words of a young East African poet, Wandera-Chagenda, the hour of death is 'zero-hour' — not only a cipher that signifies nothingness but the end of a countdown for ... what?[17] Michel Kayoya's views on death have been made more poignant by his own personal testimony.[18] For him the consciousness of death is essential to spiritual growth; it 'fashions our eternity'. Since the time of Jesus Christ, he keeps repeating, 'it is no longer difficult to die nobly'. There is no finer word with which to describe Kayoya's own bearing, when, on that May morning in 1972, the young poet-priest from Burundi, went, singing, to his death on a bridge outside Bujumbura. Laye makes his hero, Clarence, ask: 'Is this the way one dies?'[19] The final pages of *The Radiance of the King* contain Laye's anticipation of what death will be like. Silence, radiance, fire are the images he uses and the ultimate security of being swept into the cloak of the divine boy-king whose heart-beat is so faint and yet so tremendously powerful. No, death is not the negation of life; it is the end of a quest. Both Kayoya and Laye describe that quest in terms of 'hunger', 'thirst', a 'void' that longs to be filled. It is achieved only by losing oneself, by accepting one's own nakedness — by welcoming 'the thickly-feathered silence' of death.

One theme that emerges very clearly from the pages of African spiritual writers is that religion must not become an evasion of responsibility. Human beings, stresses Nyerere, must take control of their own lives, and make their own choices.[20] Marx's description of religion as an 'opium' is verified, thinks Kayoya, in the shallow religiosity of so many African Christians. Their religion blinds them to the real causes of their misfortune.[21] Instead of helping them to live in this world, their faith encourages them to escape from it. This is because the Christianity of so many adults is not merely child-like but childish. They have not learned what love really means or what human fulfilment really means in an adult world.

Human fulfilment certainly means building the earth and achieving 'maximum being', to use a favourite expression of Senghor.[22] But this does not mean putting man in the place of God. The true value of man cannot be understood, asserts Kaunda, by making him into the ultimate reality and clothing him with divine attributes. The humility of a religious believer is necessary if humanity is to develop all its resources. There is not a single one of these spiritual writers who would deny the benfits of technological development to the people of Africa, but, as Kaunda, Laye and Nyamiti express it, they want technology without materialism. God is an inner necessity for humankind.

Senghor, Kayoya, Mwoleka, Omoyajowo all reject the doctrine of Karl Marx, but the burden of their argument is not against a speculative atheism, it is against a denial of love.[23] Love personalizes; brute force and violence depersonalizes those who employ such methods. Love, according to Camara Laye, means listening, nearness and sympathy.[24] For Kayoya it is essentially what makes a human being noble.[25] For Kaunda and Senghor, love is associated with the human presence. It is the stuff of life — the power that works a fundamental change in people and makes them superior beings.[26] That is why a community or a nation that is built without love, and without the attraction of a God who is love, is a dehumanized community.

Kenneth Kaunda draws a daring conclusion from this contemplation of the world of the spirit in Africa. African-ness is itself a religious phenomenon. [27] Being an African, means being a believer. Although Kaunda in no way disguises his own strong Christian convictions, he is reluctant to identify Africa with any one religious tradition. There is a power in all faiths, and religion in Africa is a force which a statesman would be foolish to ignore or attempt to destroy. Senghor adds an important corollary. If Africans are so strongly influenced by religion, it is by a religion that preaches love.[28]

3 Man and His Integral Development

The complaint is sometimes voiced that there is very little Christology in African theological and spiritual writing, the implication being that much of this writing is a reversion to the 'natural' religion of African tradition and that it lacks the specifying Christian element — the encounter with the man, Jesus Christ. To some extent the complaint may be justified. On the other hand, it depends on the kind of Christology the complainant has in mind. Traditional Christology was a Christology 'from above'. It focussed on the Incarnation and on the theological and philosophical problems involved in the process of God becoming a man. Contemporary Christology is 'from below'. It focusses on the human existence of Jesus, the fullness and completeness of his humanity, reaching a climax at his passion and death in the faith of the apostles that God had raised him made him Lord. It attempts to answer the questions: Who is this man, Jesus? Where do we encounter him? For the one who believes, Jesus is God revealing himself in love to mankind, and he is found today, living his risen life in human beings, transforming their relationships and divinizing their hearts and minds. The emphasis is less on the process by which God became incarnate and more on the process by which we ourselves become incarnate. It is we who have to become more human, to realize to the full our human potentialities. Our spirituality must be an incarnate spirituality, leading us more and more to find God-in-Christ through our own human existence. God reveals himself in Christ, and

Christ — the unique, defining instance of a human being — leads us back to humankind. We are not allowed to remain in perpetual adoration of a shadowy, historical figure whose life seems to have little or nothing in common with the lives we lead today. Our task is to discover our fellow human beings in this Jesus Christ and to serve them in faith and love. In this way, we become more truly human ourselves in the measure in which we are configured to Christ.

The African spiritual writers we are considering are unanimous in their commitment to humanity. They are not preaching an inward-looking, spiritual development. They do not go in for 'spiritualism', as Magesa puts it; their aim is the integral development of human beings in community, enabling them to take control of their own lives and to make the right choices by themselves.[29] African Christian Spirituality begins and ends with people — people in their own world. When writers like Harry Sawyerr stress the Incarnation, they are not necessarily condemning Africa to an Incarnation-centred Christology, they are speaking about our humanization in Christ.[30] In Christ, humanity and the world are liberated and transformed through the power of his passion, death and resurrection. The great fear of Julius Nyerere is that the churches are preaching individualism, a personal religion of spiritual self-conquest and nothing more, and this is not a groundless fear. Nineteenth century missionary spirituality attributed great importance to personal piety and to the union of the soul with Jesus Christ. Piety was expressed through fidelity to rules and observances, and these were seen as a sure test of holiness. It was a defensive spirituality, though not a passive one. Often intolerant, and even bigoted, it conjured up the mental image of a great bulwark withstanding the raging sea of diabolically inspired paganism. It was also a spirituality that tended towards Manichaeism, towards the separation of spirit from matter, and disdain for the body, for feelings and emotions. This kind of spirituality achieved a great deal in the early days of the African mission, but it obviously has its limitations in an era of socio-economic development and organizational change, when technology and communications have thrown human beings from different traditions together, and made the barriers of blood, background and belief more painful to bear. If religion is not to become quickly irrelevant, the believer must be committed wholeheartedly to dialogue and the building of human solidarity. In an age of rapid material advancement, the Church cannot afford to stand aloof, but must show an interest in the whole human person, including his or her bodily existence, guiding people in the right use of material things. Humankind must be helped to fulfil its role of world-conquest, dominating the earth and not being dominated by it.

Early missionaries in Africa were very much at home at the courts of traditional chiefs and divine kings. European church history taught them the value of making 'key-converts', and with the examples of Clovis of the Franks and Ethelbert of Kent before their eyes, they began the process of evangelization from the top downwards. This worked tolerably well in the centralized kingdoms of the East African lake region, but it was not a strategy that could be applied to ethnic groups with a strong degree of social stratification, nor in highly segmented societies. Some missionaries even aspired to become chiefs themselves, as in the case of Bishop Joseph Dupont in Ubemba, Zambia, and everywhere the church spread with the help of local chiefs and headmen, many of whom even became catechists. In those days the Church, particularly the Roman Catholic Church, operated with a monarchical image. Kingship was applied in varying degrees to bishops, pope and to Christ. It was natural that missionaries should propose the title of 'chief' for Jesus Christ. As Harry Sawyerr points out, this is an unfortunate practice. African chiefs were often ritual figures with highly circumscribed powers. They were also often remote and inaccessible to their subjects. Even worse, chiefs became agents of the colonial administration and were identified with foreign oppression. For that reason chiefdoms were often abolished when an African country achieved political independence. If they survived it was usually as an unfashionable and irrelevant institution. Harry Sawyerr proposes a Biblical image which is considerably more meaningful in the present situation of Africa. Christ should be presented as 'the eldest brother', 'the first-born among many sons'. In this way emphasis is placed upon the humanity of Christ and his closeness to us, rather than on his inaccessibility and otherness. The eldest brother exercises many powers and privileges in the African family community, becoming eventually its head. Yet, in spite of this position of authority, he shares a common descent with his brothers and sisters and is a first among equals. Damian Lwasa suggests that Christ could be presented to African Christians as our 'ancestor'.[31] There is much that is positive in this suggestion, and it invokes again Christ's solidarity with humanity. However, an ancestor in Africa is a spirit, and though he is active among his living descendants for good and for ill, death intervenes between them, bestowing on the ancestor praeternatural powers that he did not enjoy in life. Religious traditions in many African ethnic groups present the Creator as 'ancestor', the one from whom all life derives. It would be more in keeping, with Christian theological symbolism, and with the emphases of modern African humanism, to reserve the title 'ancestor' for the first person of the Trinity, and to look upon Christ as 'eldest brother', rendered present through the Spirit in our fellow human beings.

Incarnation, therefore, means that Christ invites us to identify with our fellow human beings, and this, as Archbishop Zoa points out, entails a measure of desacralization.[32] The world of the spirit is also the world of bodily existence. Christian theology must be a situational theology — even a political theology, for in Africa, siding with man is siding with what Okolo calls 'diminished man'.[33] 'Christ is black' because he is essentially opposed to the exploitation of blacks by whites. The 'white Jesus' is a false image because a white-dominated world is unjust and inhuman. Christ sides with the poor and the oppressed, therefore he is black. Whiteness is unchristian, but blackness, which extends the bond of brotherhood to all humanity, is not only opposed to racism, but positively Christian. The symbols must change, say the black theologians. This is strong language, and many African spiritual writers, while agreeing with the argument, would not use this language. The young Ghanaian, who composed the prayer against racial discrimination, ends up by saying that God 'is greater than Europe and Africa'.[34] Africa belongs, not merely to Africans who are 'marked for this continent', but primarily to God.

Nevertheless, there must be a break, an 'epistemological

break', with the past. The world must be seen differently, no longer through the eyes of a white, master-race. There must be, as Nyerere repeats, a real revolution against unjust structures.[35] It is not enough to state moral principles without being committed to revolutionary action. It is not enough to practise charity on a small-scale without becoming a revolutionary Christian, trying to bring about a radical change in the large-scale relationships of humanity. Dominic Mwasaru goes even further in demanding a change in the structures of a white dominated Church, while Archbishop Zoa calls for a new attitude on the part of Christians, an attitude that makes them active and creative, bringing new institutions and new structures into existence.[36]

Several writers mention the fact that Africans have been alienated by the imposition of foreign structures. Colonialism was part of the process of dehumanization in Africa. Other writers express the fear that, unless Africans are ready with viable alternatives, the break-up of structures will bring social and spiritual havoc. We are already witnessing the break-up of the traditional African family community, the traditional village society, the traditional tribal structure. Colonial and missionary structures have partly assisted the break-up, partly cushioned Africans against the effects of the break-up. If Africans are not active and perspicacious now, complete disorientation will follow. There will not only be slums in the physical sense, but what Nyerere calls 'spiritual slums' as well. Africans must awaken to the realities of their present situation.

When words like 'dehumanization', 'exploitation' or 'oppression' are used, it is not only in the context of the race conflict in southern Africa or of the unjust and unbalanced relationships between the West and the Third World. It is also in the context of Africans exploiting and oppressing one another. This is what Kayoya calls 'another, more terrible colonization'. [37] There are plenty of local exploiters in Africa, plenty of corrupt and immoral leaders, plenty of strong men who trample brutally on the rights of their fellow human beings. Bishop Okullu, renowned for his outspokenness, equates tribalism and racism. Angrily he denounces leaders who violate the sanctity of human life and whose slaughter of human beings is greater even than the toll of animal lives in the game parks.[38] These large-scale massacres are a crime, not only against humanity, but against God in whose image humankind is created. Wandera-Chagenda, with his experience of events in Uganda, deplores the wastage of human resources — 'Let us not manufacture martyrs, unscheduled martyrs of our own kind!'[39] Kayoya, himself a victim of tribal violence, denounces the resort to violence by both Marxists and egotistic Capitalists. Brute force dehumanizes people, stupefies them. It is so easy to resort to force, but 'man is not made free by force'.[40]

Today in Africa, thinks the young poet Wandera-Chagenda, people are in Limbo — a state of inertia, weariness, and semi-human torpor. It is time for the Resurrection, the resurrection of humanity.[41] The human qualities so prized by the people of Burundi and so frequently on the lips of the martyr-priest, Kayoya, must be cultivated once more in the modern context — the virtues of dignity, nobility and integrity.[42] Only Christ can work this resurrection in us. Only he can restore our humanity and liberate us through his own passion, death and resurrection. This is the Christ whom the Church must preach. Two writers foretell the possible death of the Church in Africa.[43] It is the opinion of Nyerere that the Church will surely die if she continues to be identified with injustice in the world. For Mwasaru, the Church is doomed to die if she retains structures and symbols that are alien to the African tradition. The great vocation of the Church is reconciliation, unification, but ever here, as Omoyajowo points out, disunity among Christians is the stumbling-block.[44] If Africa and humanity are to enjoy the abundant life promised them by Jesus Christ, there must truly be a Christian Revolution.

4   Culture, a Living Tradition

The vocation of Christianity is the reconciliation, or the unification, of humankind. This definitely does not mean the
imposition of a world culture. Charles Nyamiti is perfectly
right to dismiss the prospect of a world culture as unrealis-
tic.[45] Christian reconciliation envisages a situation in
which people of different cultures can exchange their different experiences and traditions, even their different under-
standings of the same Jesus Christ, the Jesus Christ of the
Gospels and of Church tradition. A universal or Catholic
Church is one to which many cultures contribute. It is not
the imposition of a worldwide Christian culture which is a
shallow disguise for western culture. Respect for humanity
means 'nearness' or 'localness'.[46] As Kayoya puts it, to
respect a man is 'to draw near' and 'to listen'.[47] Culture is a
part of the human person — a person's way of life or mode
of being. Culture involves what a person thinks is important — his values. In the colonial period Africans were made
to feel ashamed of their culture. They were made to accept
alien values and alien ways. They were completely passive.[48] Their very being was conferred on them from outside'.[49] Today there must be a complete break with the
mentality of the past, with the inferiority complex of Africans in the colonial period. A deep decolonization must take
place at the level of culture.

Whereas some writers still speak of 'Christianizing African traditions', others speak of 'Africanizing Christianity'.[50]
These two phrases unconsciously reflect different images of

the Christian Church. The former sees the Church as culturally unified, the latter sees the Church as a plurality in
unity, a fellowship of local churches, exchanging among
themselves their vision of the Risen Christ in a bond of
faith, hope and love. It is not simply a question of finding in
African traditions factors which are consonant with Christianity, but of being prepared to go much further than this.
We are back again at the concept of Incarnation, for Christianity must become incarnate in African cultures. Christ is
present in every human situation, in every community and
every human tradition, and this fact must be rendered explicit. Africans must experience Christ in their own communities and within their own cultural traditions; they are not
asked to react to someone else's experience of Christ.

In this connection, the theological pilgrimage of the
Roman Catholic Church is instructive. In the early days of
this century when missionaries were just beginning to take
a more positive attitude towards the religious traditions of
non-Christians, it was fashionable to speak of the *praeparatio evangelii*, the 'preparation for the Gospel'. In Africa,
Christian writers even sometimes spoke of 'Africa's Old
Testament'. The idea was that Africans had been providen-
tially prepared for the proclamation of the Gospel by their
own religious tradition. This was their 'Old Testament' —
not, of course, in the sense that it could replace the Jewish
Old Testament, but in the sense that non-Christian traditions were analogous to the Jewish Old Testament. The
implication was that, once the Gospel had been effectively
proclaimed, there was no further need for the non-Christian
tradition. It had been completely superseded.

To the concept of *praeparatio evangelii* succeeded the concept of 'adaptation'. This is a word which one still hears
quite frequently on Roman Catholic lips, and the idea
which it represents underlies much of the Church's centralized legislation. The idea is that there is a basic blueprint for
theology, worship, morality, religious education and so on
throughout the universal Church. Texts may be translated
into vernaculars and superficial alterations can be made but
these do not affect the essential. Adaptation is a one-way process. Decisions are taken centrally and handed down to the
local churches for translation. All eyes are glued to the origi-

nal text which must be faithfully rendered in the vernacular. The result is usually a lifeless thing, owing more to western than to African forms, or neutral to the point of inanity.

Finally, the Second Vatican Council proclaimed a new ideal which cannot be said to have been implemented yet, although the Bishops of Africa and Madagascar and Pope Paul VI have declared themselves in favour of it on various occasions.[51] This is the concept of 'Incarnation' or, as the missionary decree of the Second Vatican Council puts it, 'the seeds of the Word'. Christ is at work in non-Christian traditions and he has planted seeds there, authentic Christian elements which the (African) Christian must recognize and put to use. Traditional culture must be carefully examined and the seeds of the Word must be uncovered 'with gladness and respect'. Nothing must be allowed to be lost which can 'praise the glory of the Creator, manifest the grace of the Saviour, or contribute to the right ordering of Christian life'. In other words, eyes must be focussed on local culture, and local churches must be creative. Moreover, it is not simply a search for elements in African tradition that parallel those in cultures already Christianized. Seeds will be recognized and cultivated that will grow into flowers hitherto unknown in the garden of the Church, because African Christians will be prompted by their own culture and tradition to ask new questions of the Gospel and to see Christ in a new light.

It is for this reason that African Christian writers call for creativity.[52] Some go so far as to ask for African rites and an African methodology for Religious Education. Moral judgements also must be realistic and reflect the social situation of African Christians. It is simply not possible to have a single blueprint for these things, a blueprint that can be imposed on the entire Church. Nor is it ultimately useful to have a worldwide theological system which can be the meeting-ground for the insights that derive from different Christian cultures. This would be an artificial construct, a kind of 'Esperanto' that belongs to nobody. What must happen, and what these writers are demanding, is the development of an ecclesial communion that favours an exchange of ideas (even though it be in translation), rather than the sacrifice of a people's own symbols and categories of thought.

Dominic Mwasaru refers to the African intellectuals who bitterly attack Christianity for its clash with African Traditional Religion and its suppression of African culture.[53] True, these intellectuals are basically ignorant of the new, dynamic image of the Church, but they base their critique on what they can see. They see local churches in Africa becoming docile, carbon copies of churches in the West. It is time, cries Mwasaru, for a radical break.

A note of warning is sounded by Omoyajowo who fears a possible revival of pre-Christian paganism.[54] This is certainly a danger but it is more likely to be the outcome of a refusal to enter into dialogue with African religious traditions than of a conscious encounter with them.

Another fear is that of archaism, the fear that the Church, in trying to become more African, will revert to a moribund culture that has no relevance in the modern situation. Charles Nyamiti does not share this fear. African tradition is a living tradition, and the African past is a source of creative impulses and new beginnings, not an era that is dead and forgotten. He notes how, in the history of Europe and the western world, creativity has always been linked with renaissance and the recovery or reinterpretation of a past culture. "Roots' are important to the African intelligentsia, and this is a fact which the Church ignores at her peril. Moreover, as Kenneth Kaunda and Camara Laye pointed out, rural Africa is closer to the past, and ninety per cent of modern Africa is rural. Christianity has to come to terms with the cultural revival in Africa, or face extinction like the colonial, Latin church of Carthage and north Africa.

A concept which, perhaps, the African spiritual writers do not exploit sufficiently is that of memorial, or effective memory.[56] This concept is present in most of the religious systems of the world, although it is stronger in those with a highly developed sense of history. It is certainly visible in many of the religious traditions of Africa. By remembering past events and places, particularly by imitating the actions of the ancestors when they walked the earth, one can secure the favour of God. The ancestors won God's favour in their day; now the living declare their solidarity with them, using the same formulas and making their offerings in the same holy places. Christianity has to discover a real continuity with the African religious past, if Africans are to feel that it is their religion, and not a foreign import. It is significant that in newly drafted Eucharistic rites in Zaïre and Tanzania, the ancestors are invoked and invited to be witnesses of the liturgical action.

Laurenti Magesa and Raymond Arazu underline another area of possible continuity between African Traditional Religion and African Christianity.[57] This is the area of types or styles of praying. Magesa rightly maintains that African traditional prayer was characterized by a large measure of spontaneity, and it was Heiler, the socio-psychologist of prayer, who called it 'primary prayer', on the grounds that spontaneous prayer is closer to the real feelings and actual religious experience of the worshipper. Magesa calls for a much greater freedom in Christian public worship, for spontaneous praying and for a free choice of texts, instead of always being dominated by a book. Arazu stresses the need for individual contemplation to enable Christians to know God in his image which is the human body-spirit. Undoubtedly, there is evidence of a contemplative tradition in pre-Christian Africa and Arazu offers us a good instance of it in the Ozo initiation rituals of the Igbo in Nigeria. The Ozo initiant had to contemplate his own divinely given nature, and Christians must do the same in order to obtain an understanding of God.

There is certainly a need in modern African Christianity for spontaneity and for depth in prayer. The growing popularity of charismatic worship in the independent churches, and even in the mission churches, is evidence of this. Perhaps, the most far-reaching attempt to create a charismatic, African Christianity was that of Placide Tempels in the 1950s.[58] The spiritual movement which he launched in Zaïre (then the Congo) was a practical application of ideas he had popularized in his *Bantu Philosophy* a few years earlier.[59] It was known by the Swahili name *jamaa*, 'family' — not to be confused with *ujamaa*, 'familyhood', the political philosophy of Tanzania. The movement was based on the three fundamental aspirations of the Bantu which Tempels had identified: desire for life, desire for vital union with the sources of life, and fecundity or the transmission of life. There were to be no rules, manuals, or instructions. *Jamaa* was an idea, a spirit of encounter and mutual self-revelation between priests and laity. Spiritual 'families' were to be set up, based on a free exchange of ideas, dreams and feelings, and on shared prayer. Married Christians were to transcend their physical communion of life by realizing a deeper communion in God, the source of life. They were, as a third stage, then to transmit spiritual life by 'fathering' and 'mothering' other *jamaa* members, and even a priest, in a session, in which a member of the clergy made a kind of personal confession to them.

Tempels constantly repudiated any idea that he was the leader of the *jamaa* movement, but in actual fact the movement was not able to survive his departure from Africa — at lease in its desired form. The ideas behind *jamaa* were too abstract to make an appeal to people except in the poly-ethnic urban and mining areas where a substitute for traditional culture was needed. The movement attracted few priests and, consequently, the third stage of spiritual development was seldom attained. The movement became more structured, and a fair amount of formal instruction was introduced. Much of the latter employed sensual imagery, with the result that a heterdox shadow-*jamaa* came into existence, practising sexual communalism, and the movement as a whole was censured by ecclesiastical authorities in several areas. Perhaps, one should not expect a charismatic movement to outlive its founder and risk becoming a normative community. If it is to remain truly charismatic, it should expect to disappear and be replaced by another spontaneous activity. Spontaneity in the established Christian churches of Africa depends on widespread creativity, on encouragement from church authorities and on a formula for worship and instruction that balances spontaneity and formality. Charismatic movements tend to go to extremes and to constitute a threat to organized churches if this balance is not achieved. Magesa and Arazu are therefore right to demand a greater measure of spontaneity in regular Christian worship as a creative link with African religious tradition.

5 The Human Community

T.S. Eliot wrote about men's fear,

> Their fear of fear and frenzy, their fear of possession,
> Of belonging to another, or to others, or to God.[60]

Community is the capacity to overcome this fear. It is the willingness of human beings to belong to one another in love. This is how Kenneth Kaunda sees the tradition of community living in Africa.[61] We have already noted his ideas about the community dimension of the human soul, the soul as the seat of social virtue, or the primal essence of man at the centre of a network of social relationships. Let us examine his picture of society. African traditional community was a mutual society. That meant that human need was the criterion of behaviour. Members of the community acted always to fulfil a human need, their own and that of others. They co-operated because there was strength in numbers and this was the only effective way of supplying the need. African traditional community was an accepting society, because it offered support, particularly to its weaker members, the old and the handicapped. Perhaps the greatest value in community living is the support it offers. It is not a question of mutual admiration or of making mutual demands, but of mutual acceptance and of going through things together. In a really accepting community one does not expect too much of one another. Certainly one does not give ultimatums to others. One accepts. Finally, according to Kaunda, African traditional community was an inclusive society. By that is meant that responsibility was shared very widely. For example, a wide range of relatives, neighbours and villagers shared responsibility for the education and discipline of young children. Or again, the demands of hospitality were far-reaching, extending not only to the whole family community, but to clan, chiefdom and, on occasion, the whole ethnic or language group.

Kaunda is not alone in regretting the disruption of this traditional community life in Africa, a disruption brought about by the processes of social change. Bernadette Kunambi also points to the disruption of society.[62] Feelings are mixed, because there is so much that is good and so much that is inevitable in this world of change; but Africa is not coping with it very successfully. Community life can no longer be taken for granted. The old ideal must be consciously proclaimed and steps taken to make it applicable to the modern situation. The basic community must be rediscovered and articulated within the life of a modern nation-state. This is Kaunda's hope. For Nyerere, it is more than a hope or an ideal; it is the basis of a programme of action — a programme of action known to the world as *ujamaa* ('familyhood').

The policy of *ujamaa* is well known. Its aim is to help ordinary people take control of their own lives, therefore it involves regionalization or decentralization. People must be encouraged to live and work together in villages in a real, family spirit of co-operation, sharing and trust. It is not a form of villagization which encourages individual settlers to become richer than their fellows. Rather, inequalities must be strongly discouraged, so that the whole community develops together at the same pace, without any classes coming into existence. *Ujamaa* has no hard and fast philosophy behind it. It is essentially pragmatic, realizing the ideal step by step, by trial and error. Inevitably, *ujamaa* is severely judged on economic grounds, but, clearly also, economics is subordinate to social goals in Tanzania. The aim of development is the human community, and its well-being and solidarity come before the material standard of living. Egotism, whether individual or collective, is the great enemy.

Ujamaa is an excellent starting-point for a discussion of the Christian meaning of community. Both Bishop Mwoleka and Camillus Lyimo approach it from this point of view.[63] For Mwoleka, Christians have a moral obligation to seize the opportunity offered by *ujamaa*, and to provide the interior dispositions, the internal strength, needed to make it a success. God is the goal of human life and God, himself, is a Trinitarian community. This is not a theological dogma to be pondered intellectually (ultimately, without comprehension); it is a truth to be lived. Life on earth is a rehearsal for the celestial community. Heaven begins here and now, and Christians must make it apparent, not only by sharing their earthly goods, but by becoming completely 'other-centred'. For Lyimo, '*ujamaa* theology' is a programme of love-centred action, which helps humankind achieve its potential through interaction. It is a call to peaceful world-conquest. It is a prophetical movement, because it is not afraid to criticize or be criticized. Once again — no starry-eyed idealism, but a practical realism!

The traditional African community was not a community of the living only. It was a community of both the living and the dead. Death was somehow swallowed up in the affirmation of a vital relationship between ancestors and descendants. Both Sawyerr and Lwasa speak of this phenomenon and discuss its relevance to African Christian Community.[64] Sawyerr appeals to the doctrine of the Communion of Saints and the Christian belief that God's Spirit renews and gives life to the whole of humanity. The pre-Christian ancestors who never heard the name of Christ in their lifetimes, reach their perfection in company with the present Christian generation. Lwasa, speaking from the Ganda experience (Uganda), emphasizes the traditional African belief in the immortality of the soul, and he extends the idea of a solidarity between living and departed family members to the whole Mystical Body of Christ. The African family, extended in space and time, becomes an apt image of the whole human community, redeemed by Christ. Christ is the norm of life for this family, as are the ancestors for the African family, and the Spirit is the principle of life that he bequeaths to those who are his family members. Lwasa takes a highly positive approach to African culture, speaking of the Christian Gospel as itself a seed, nourished in the African soil by cultural elements. This image of the seed falls short of the *semina verbi*, 'the seeds of the Word', another use of the same image by the Missionary Decree (*Ad Gentes*) of the Second Vatican Council.

Christian evangelization, however, has not always contributed positively to the building of the human community in Africa. Bernadette Kunambi makes this point.[65] African Church history has been a history of disunity and division imported by the Christian churches of Europe and America into Africa. Africans have learned the prejudices all too readily, living, as they do, in ignorance of the real facts or of the real causes of division. Ecumenical action is, therefore, necessarily a part of Christian community-building in Africa today. Contacts have to be multiplied, practical co-operation between churches at all levels must be encouraged, so that effective communion is restored. Theologians in the different churches are daily drawing closer to one another. Leaders are mutually well disposed, but church denominations are still held in ignorance of one another, and are still prejudiced against work for Christian unity.

Bernadette Kunambi deals with the social position of women, and Lyimo also refers to this question in passing. There is no doubt that women occupied an inferior position in African traditional society, but so, too, did they in the structures of the Christian Church. Today, the woman's lot has been made even more unbearable. The Church has shared in the movement to educate and emancipate women in Africa, but there has been no parallel development in the social and ecclesial structures themselves. Women are therefore increasingly prepared for a role that they are not allowed to play. Discrimination becomes more acutely felt, and women are increasingly tempted to seek alternative lifestyles, outside the ordinary institutions of marriage, family and church community. Our spiritual writers, as a whole, are hardly conscious of the problem. Sexist language is second nature to them, because — it must be admitted — they are often translating Bantu terms which, like *muntu*, 'human being', have no sexist overtones, but which, in English, they render as 'man'. However, be that as it may, there are no signs of any sensitivity to the problem of discrimination. Even Julius Nyerere confessed recently that it was President Jimmy Carter who had taught him to say: 'One person, one vote', instead of 'One man, one vote'. Bernadette Kunambi ends her contribution with the impassioned plea to the Church to cease treating women as 'second or third-class citizens'. African and Christian thinking about the human community will have to take up this challenge.

Community virtues were taught to the young African through initiation ceremonies at puberty. Parents and children co-operated in this all-important institution. Children felt the concern and support of the parental generation as they prepared to enter upon the adult state of life. As in all rites of passage, there was a threshold moment or 'liminal' period, when they were neither children nor adults. They were suspended, as it were, between the two conditions. It was then that they learned the real nature of community, the real basis of their shared humanity. It was then that society inscribed its ideals on their hearts and minds, as on a blank page. This condition of 'liminality', as the anthropologist Victor Turner calls it, was a memory that lasted all their lives, a bond that drew the age-mates together more closely than ties of blood. [66] It was an experience that people in later life constantly sought to recapture through secret societies, masked dances and other rituals. Christianity has to impart a 'liminal quality' to the human community, helping people to live intensely, rediscover their common humanity, and hold before their eyes the ideals which can only ultimately be realized in the heavenly condition, when all human beings will share in the community of God.

References to Part One

1. This introduction makes use of a paper presented by the editor to the consultation on 'Christianity in Independent Africa', held at Jos Campus, Nigeria, in September 1975. The paper, entitled 'Developments in African Christian Spirituality', is due to appear in the record of the Jos Consultation, being edited by Fr. Adrian Hastings. At the time of writing, this work has not been published.

2. The editor has been closely associated with the making of two syllabuses of this type. They are the Secondary School Religion Syllabuses prepared at the AMECEA Pastoral Institute (Gaba), known as *Developing in Christ* (1973) and *Christian Living Today* (1974), both published by Geoffrey Chapman.

3. Cf. Part Two, no. 4.

4. The editor has attempted to do this in *African Christian Theology* (Geoffrey Chapman, 1975), chap. 3, p. 38 ff.

5. The Roman Catholic Bishops of Kenya, Malawi, Tanzania, Uganda, Zambia, Ethiopia and Sudan, in their episcopal association known as AMECEA, have been particularly preoccupied with the question of Christian community building in the last four years. In 1977 the Roman Catholic Bishops of Zimbabwe (Rhodesia) also launched a programme of Christian community building.

6. Cf. Part Two, no. 1.

7. Cf. Part Two, no. 28.

8. Cf. Victor Turner, *The Ritual Process* (Chicago, 1969); Joseph Goetz (with F.M. Bergounioux) *Prehistoric and Primitive Religions* (London, 1965).

9. For example, Jean-Claude Bajeux, 'Mentalité noire et mentalité biblique', in *Des Prêtres Noirs S'Interrogent* (Paris, 1956) pp. 57-82; Bonganjalo Goba, 'Corporate Personality: Ancient Israel and Africa', in Basil Moore, ed., *Black Theology* (London, 1973), pp. 65-73. This subject is treated in detail in the editor's 'Africa's Old Testament' in the *Africa Service Bulletin* of the World Catholic Federation for the Biblical Apostolate, no. 22. It also appeared in that organization's *The Biblical Apostolate* 7, no. 2: 56-57.

10. Harold Turner, 'A Typology for African Religious Movements', *Journal of Religion in Africa* no. 1: 1-34.

11. Cf. nos. 1, 2 and 3 of PartTwo.

12. Cf. no. 7 of Part Two.

13. Cf. Part Two, nos. 1 and 8.

14. Cf. Part Two, nos. 1, 2 and 28.

15. Alexis Kagame, *La Philosophie Bantu Comparée* (Paris, 1976), pp. 210-18.

16. John 10:10, quoted in nos. 14 and 29 of Part Two.

17. Part Two, no. 6.

18. Part Two, no. 2.

19. Part Two, no. 7.

20. Part Two, no. 14.

21. Part Two, no. 4.

22. Part Two, no. 5.

23. Part Two, nos. 4, 15, 18 and 25.

24. Part Two, no. 1.

25. Part Two, no. 2.

26. Part Two, nos. 3 and 5.

27. Part Two, no. 3.

28. Part Two, no. 5.

29. Part Two, nos. 11 and 14.

30. Part Two, no. 8.

31. Part Two, no. 29.

32. Part Two, no. 12.

33. Part Two, no. 9.

34. Part Two, no. 10.

35. Part Two, no. 14.

36. Part Two, nos. 12 and 19.

37. Part Two, no. 15.

38. Part Two, no. 16.

39. Part Two, no. 17.

40. Part Two, no. 15.

41. Part Two, no. 13.

42. Part Two, no. 15.

43. Part Two, nos. 14 and 19.

44. Part Two, no. 18.

45. Part Two, no. 20.

46. Cf. Aylward Shorter, *African Christian Theology* (Geoffrey Chapman, London, 1975), pp. 145-61, where there is a discussion about theology in a multi-cultural church.

47. Part Two, no. 2.

48. Several writers make this point, but particularly Archbishop Zoa. See Part Two, no. 12.

49. Words spoken by Cardinal Paul Zoungrana at the opening of the first Roman Catholic Symposium of African Bishops in Uganda in July 1969.

50. Pope Paul VI on his visit to Africa in 1969, first used the phrase 'an African Christianity'.

51. *Ad Gentes* (Decree of the Church's Missionary Activity), no. 22. Report of 1974 Rome Synod *AMECEA Documentation Service*, no. 11/74/2, pp. 2-3. Paul VI's 'Closing Discourse to All-Africa Symposium', *Gaba Pastoral Paper*, no. 7, pp. 50-51.

52. Part Two, no. 12.

53. Part Two, no. 19.

54. Part Two, no. 18.

55. Part Two, no. 20.

56. For a fuller treatment of this theme see Aylward Shorter, *African Christian Theology* (Geoffrey Chapman, London, 1975), pp. 113-17.

57. Part Two, nos. 22 and 23. Cf. also F. Heiler, *Prayer* (London, 1932).

58. The following account of the *jamaa* movement is based on Temple's own writings, chiefly in *Notre Rencontre* (Leopoldville, 1962) and on Johannes Fabian's *Jamaa* (Evanston, 1971). A very detailed account of *jamaa* was also published in 1977 by Willy de Craemer, *Jamaa and the Church* (Oxford University Press).

59. Cf. Placide Tempels, *La Philosophie Bantoue* (Elizabethville, 1945).

60. T.S. Eliot, 'East Coker' in *Four Quartets* (London, 1968) pp. 24-25.

61. Part Two, no. 28.

62. Part Two, no. 30.

63. Part Two, nos. 25 and 26.

64. Part Two, nos. 27 and 29.

65. Part Two, no. 30.

66. Victor Turner, *op. cit.*

Part Two
Readings in African Christian Spirituality

First Commitment: A World of the Spirit

1 The Soul of Africa
Camara Laye

Camara Laye is a well-known writer from French-speaking Africa. Although his background is a Muslim one, he has been strongly affected by the culture and religion of France where he has lived a great part of his life. In his celebrated book The African Child *he sought to recapture the experiences of his own childhood in his native Guinea. In the passage that follows he explains to an African Writer's Conference the importance of his childhood as the symbol of a spiritual world. Camara Laye's impassioned credo is one of the best statements of the traditional belief which is the heritage also of Christian writers in Africa.*

Yesterday in Africa we were nearer to beings and things, and that for reasons which are not at all mysterious. Perhaps it was only because our life was less busy and we ourselves less distracted. We were shielded by having fewer artificial elements in our lives, fewer facilities. Our towns cut us off less from the country. We lived like the men of the Middle Ages, knowing nothing or almost nothing of this mechanical age, the age Europe and America are passing through.

Do not, however, on any account confuse — as is only too often done — this mechanical age with civilization itself. Civilization is something quite different. It is not to be confused with machinery and still less with bombs and interplanetary missiles. Civilization, European, American, Asian and our own, existed long before mechanical progress. Not that Africa despises mechanical progress. On the contrary, she longs for it, but regards it as merely an accessory to real civilization.

Man's body has its needs, but so has his soul, and the soul, after all, comes before the body, however little the two can be separated and however little the body is to be despised.

In large towns, the accumulation of mechanical aids can easily smother the soul which is, as it were, borne down by all kinds of progress which are not its concern, but the effects of which it can rarely escape. But the soul knows what is happening. It feels its chains and seeks by every means to shake them off. Some of the ways it tries are as odd,

I feel sure, as any to be found in our old beliefs that yesterday so surprised the European rationalists.

We must, however, be careful not to mistake the nature of their rationalism, which exists far more in their speech than in their thought. When we look at what is best and most genuine in Europe, it is not machinery that we see but books, paintings, architecture; what our ears hear is not the humming of machinery but the sound of orchestras. What is truly deep and genuine in Europe is the message of her writers and artists, her scientists, moralists, musicians and revolutionaries. That is Europe's soul and the message is not one of rationalism. It is a message coming from the soul and nowhere else. That is true, despite the signs of rationalism to be discerned in the so-called abstract works of certain artists and musicians in Europe today; signs, moreover, which it would be hard to discern in any of her writers, because while the abstract can creep into painting and music, in literature it is revealed for what it is — complete emptiness.

You will be wondering what all this digression has been leading us to. It has simply been leading us back again to the mystery which is indissolubly linked to the soul, the invisible without which the soul could not exist in us. It has brought us back to that union between heaven and earth which we share with all civilizations and from which they all take their rise.

When writing my childhood memories, I wanted them to lead me on to the ineffable, to the minute and patient search for the ineffable which is the concern of us all — the search which directs us beyond the surroundings of this mechanical age, which ties us all to the same destiny, the destiny of all human beings, none of whom are more than travellers in this world. Although my ambition far out-ran my powers, that was what I was trying to do when I decided my book should relate all the mystery inherent in my childhood memories.

In the past, in the great over-grown villages of Kouroussa in Upper Guinea, there is no doubt that the air, water, earth and savannahs were really and truly inhabited by genii who had to be propitiated by prayers and sacrifices. There really were people who could bewitch you, and there were formulas for averting the ill effects of their charms. There were innumerable amulets that could be worn for protection. There were tellers of hidden things, there were healers, some of whom really effected cures. All these things really did exist, surprised as our children and grandchildren will be to learn it. All these things were current yesterday in Africa and they greatly astonished the Europeans, although they then possessed their own mysteries which, though they were different, should nevertheless have taught them to accept the existence of ours.

Everything I wrote down, everything I remembered, was a really true picture.

And why should it not be true?

Is there nothing to the world except what we can see at a casual glance?

Does not the true reality of the world consist precisely in what cannot be seen at a glance?

Is life everything?

Is death nothing?

Has life nothing behind it?

Does death finish everything?

Is death at the end of everything?

Think what a life would be that was to be finished by death! Think what a vast swindle our life and all its activity would be! Is such a swindle conceivable? I refuse to believe it. Our soul refuses to believe it. And so it is with all the rest that I prefer to believe in, however surprising it may seem to us when we happen to think of it in our worser moments, when we are no longer ourselves, when our soul ceases to vibrate, and our whole being becomes sluggish, or is animated by some unreasoning or over-reasoning logic.

My whole being cries for wonders, for prodigies, and when I recognize their presence I know that it is the better part of myself awakening, my whole self.

The visible world shrinks suddenly before my eyes; I watch it dwindling into what it is, a dream and yet not quite a dream. But the sign, the sign of what exists beyond, of what is higher, infinitely higher, than the sign which itself is only appearance, is nothing, nothing that can satisfy. . . . I see the invisible rise up and confound our poor little reason which can only claim so tiny a place; I see the inexplicable elevated once more to its seat which is supreme above all.

At last I see the soul! . . . I recognize the soul!

And I know that there are more things, many more things, in heaven than those we are aware of on earth.

2 Rediscovery
Michel Kayoya

Michel Kayoya was a young Roman Catholic priest from Burundi. His first book My Father's Footprints *is a prose-poem in which he measures his experience of Western Capitalist and Communist societies against the way of life bequeathed to him by his own parents, and finds the foreign systems wanting. For him, a truly human life consists in fidelity to his own culture, developed and perfected by Christianity. To get the most out of life, one must live with the consciousness of death. One must be prepared to die nobly. Not only — as Camara Laye insists — is death not the end; it is the fulfilment of all that one lives and longs for. Michel Kayoya was one of the priests executed by firing-squad in the tribal conflict that raged in Burundi in 1972.*

Man is born to die.
You appear among men
You stir things up for a short time
And then pass on,
Men glide by and die,
Others are born, live and glide by
As long as man is not conscious of death
He dreams, thinks, invents, builds and believes he is great
As long as man is not conscious of death
He forgets that he is not conscious and that he will die
He is ambitious for everything, and believes himself
to be the 'vital link' in a world where he leaves but few traces
Hardly has he awakened than he is gone!
He passes by
He dares to laugh, to rejoice, to fall into despair
He dares to eat, to sleep while he is on the way
While he journeys towards the unknown.

Do you understand that, my good man?
What are you doing about your awakening and your noble death?
Since the coming of Jesus Christ it is no longer difficult to

die nobly
Jesus Christ!
Do you know him?
You know his history
His influence on history
His importance in history
You are happy when you can unravel what he said
When you know how to describe his deeds
You know his history and the legends that the man in the
street has added to it
Yes, you know it
Man of little worth!
You forget that you did not know him
You philosophize, discuss, study,
Unveil him like some curious object
Is that what you call knowing?
To know, to draw nearer in silence, to listen
To draw nearer, to listen, to sympathize
To know, first to be convinced of one's ignorance.
To have a void
A thirst
To have a thirst, a void which longs to be filled
You know nothing at all!
Have you read the little book they call the Gospel?
Have you settled down to read ten times over that little
book they call the Gospel?
Little man, do you know Jesus Christ?
Do you know that he is living and that he sees?
He sees you, he looks at you
What will you do when you come across such a love as
you have never dreamed of welcoming?
Since the coming of Jesus Christ it is no longer difficult to
love nobly
We are born to die
We die in order to live
We are born, we live, we pass by
We live, as we pass by,
Passing by, we fashion our eternity.

3 The Religious Phenomenon of African-ness
Kenneth Kaunda

Kenneth Kaunda, President of the Republic of Zambia, is a Christian statesman of the first rank in Africa and the world. In this letter written to his own children he recalls the uncomplicated faith of his childhood, as the son of a Presbyterian pastor. Not only does Kaunda believe that the spiritual dimension is part of the human personality; he asserts that it is pre-eminently a part of the African personality. Zambian Humanism, the political philosophy which he has given to his country, rests on the premise that Man is the paramount creation of God.

The Africanness which has its roots in the soil of our continent rather than the lecture rooms of Western universities is basically a religious phenomenon; we are who we are because of our attitude to the mysterious depth in life, symbolized by birth and death, harvest and famine, ancestors and the unborn.

The coming of Christianity had a complex effect on this African world view, partly disrupting and partly enlarging it. I don't want to get bogged down in all that business though. It is enough to say that I feel within myself the tension created by the collision of these two world views which I have never completely reconciled. It is a ludicrous and indeed insulting over-simplification to claim, as some missionaries have done, that we non-Western peoples are still deep down pagan with a top dressing of Christianity. The same could, of course, be said of Jesus who, after all, was a middle-eastern peasant. The more sensitive theologians are beginning to explore what it means to be a Christian in a genuinely African or Asian way. I wish some of our own African clergy showed more interest in this complex problem and put a little less zeal into turning their congregations into black versions of seventeenth century English Puritans.

However — here endeth a lecture on which I ought never

to have embarked. My parents taught me to believe in God, and I have been a man of faith ever since. That is not the same thing as saying I have always been a righteous man. That is for God and my fellow men to judge. But religious faith has played a central role in my life, and even at the price of being considered old-fashioned or naive I must declare the fact. I believe in a Supreme Being whose love is the great driving force working itself out in those three worlds which interpenetrate each other at any moment of time, the worlds of Nature, History and Eternity. For me, God is more a Presence than a philosophical concept. I am aware, even in solitude, that I am not alone; that my cries for help or comfort or strength are heard. Above all, my belief in God gives me a feeling of unlimited responsibility. What a terrifying thing that is! I am guardian rather than owner of such powers and talents as I possess, answerable for my use or abuse of them to the One who has loaned them to me and will one day require a full reckoning. This sense of responsibility seems to be a great burden but at least it frees me from worrying too much about popularity or fame.

By modern standards, the religion of my parents would seem crude and oversimple. They believed that every last word of the Bible was divinely inspired; that to break any one of the Ten Commandments must consign the transgressor after death to a real Hell unless he were saved by the blood of Jesus. And they lived expecting the return in glory of Jesus and his angels to begin the judgement. There was nothing sophisticated about their faith, but it was real, strong and wholesome. And it was a Gospel with power which changed men. There was power in my mother's prayers and in my father's preaching and in our lusty hymn-singing. When those Lubwa Christians sang the old chorus — 'There is power, power, wonderworking power in the blood of the Lamb' — they meant it. And they could point to members of their family, neighbours and friends who had been brought to Jesus and freed from all the dark forces of evil and superstition which never seemed far from the surface of the old life. My father died when I was eight years of age and no one who was part of the great congregation who attended his funeral could doubt the reality of Eternity.

Colin Morris has written somewhere that the first twenty

minutes of any speech I make is more like a sermon than a
political oration. Whether he meant that comment as a com-
pliment or criticism I don't know, but it is true in the sense
that my style must have been influenced by the passionate
preaching I so often heard in my youth. It was this power of
the Gospel which enabled humble, and often unlettered village men to stand in the pulpit of the old brick church at
Lubwa and speak with tongues of fire. They had passion,
real passion, a quality noticeably lacking in much modern
preaching — which is more likely to consist of a bout of mor-
alizing about world affairs or some agile juggling with intellectual propositions which chase each other's tails until the
congregation is dizzy.

To be honest I no longer find my parents' faith satisfying.
There is nothing strange about that. After all, my world is
more complex than the one they knew. I have travelled the
globe, in the Far East, Asia, Europe and the Americas, let
alone Africa, and felt the impact of other cultures and religions. This rich experience has led me to question, reassess
and add to my youthful beliefs. Nevertheless, I do not repudi-
ate what my parents taught me about God. It is as much a
part of me as the colour of my eyes or the texture of my skin.
Indeed, it never ceases to amaze me how, in moments of crisis, I revert instinctively to the passionate simplicty of the
old religion. When the crunch comes, it is often the trustful
prayers of my childhood I find upon my lips. And even now,
I have only to hear some of those old hymns of my Lubwa
days and tears spring to my eyes. Let sophisticates sneer at
such sentimentality. It is something much deeper — a turning in on my roots; the desire to share the certainty and assur-
ance of those village Christians — the hope against hope
that the God they never doubted will not let me down either
in my hour of need.

So now you understand why I insist on family prayers,
grace at table and, whenever possible, the daily reading
together of the Bible. I am well aware of a certain degree of
rebelliousness amongst you. And I also know that there is a
school of thought which deplores the forcing of a parent's
religion down his children's throats. 'Let children make up
their own minds about religion', say such experts. That
seems to me utter rubbish. Ought we to allow children to

make up their minds whether they will steal or be honest, tell the truth or become habitual liars? Do we allow them to decide whether they will learn to read and write? It is for parents to pass on to children the fruits of their experience, and if God is the most important reality in a parent's life, then he has a duty to explain to his children why this is so and what it has all meant to him.

Further, I am convinced that the spiritual dimension is an integral part of the human personality. If it is not developed, it does not disappear but becomes warped and degenerate. And this can be just as destructive in later life as a deformed moral sense. Of course I am opposed to that kind of religious teaching which is an insult to the child's intelligence — the parrot-like repetition of propositions about God which the developing mind will easily and rightly demolish, resulting in bewilderment or cynicism. I personally believe that it is the child's sense of mystery which has to be encouraged. This is the heart of all true religion. The teaching and all the rest of it is secondary — not unimportant but secondary. Possibly the single most important distinction the human mind must learn to make is that between the unknown and the unknowable. The advance of learning will reduce the area of the unknown, given time, but the unknowable is forever beyond its scope — it is that element of mystery at the heart of everything, from simple objects like a blade of grass to profound realities such as sacrificial love.

If, when you are mature, you wish to reject what I have taught you about God, so be it. But I am determined that it is good religion that you may turn your backs on: the best I am capable of teaching you. There is no more moral choice involved in rejecting bad religion than bad music or art. That is a matter of taste, not of moral choice. But to come to the conclusion that God does not exist; that the great religions have for thousands of years been perpetuating a fantasy — that requires a truly heroic decision, for atheism is not without its difficulties and hardships. Meanwhile, we shall continue to explore the Faith together. They say that if you learn to swim when a child and then fall into a river twenty years later, the strokes will come back to you instinctively. It is in this light I see the teaching of religion to children. So that if you feel the need of God in later life, you will have some idea where to look for him. Believe me, there are many things children find a drag and a bore and would gladly abandon, but it is very difficult in later life trying to regain that early lost ground.

I ought to add just a word about the relationship between religion and Zambian Humanism. What form that Humanism will take as the years wear on, I cannot know. I certainly do not regard myself as a philosopher permanently enriching the world's thought systems, but rather as a practical man confronted with a serious challenge and feeling my way towards a response. Historically, in the West, humanism has been an alternative to the supernatural interpretation of life. Western humanists, confident in the power and truth of science, rejected theistic religion, putting Man in God's place as the ultimate reality. That was a brave thing to do, but it is far removed from my understanding of humanism which asserts the value of Man without attempting to clothe him in Divine attributes. My problem was this. Zambia is a country of many religions — Christianity, Judaism, Animism, Hinduism and Islam, and others. I did not feel it was my place as President of the new Republic to adjudicate between them, to declare this religion or that 'official' so far as the state is concerned. Each has the right to exist, and it is my desire that believers of all faiths should live together in harmony. We are, after all, human beings. We certainly cannot afford to add religious divisions to the tribal differences which threaten our national unity. There is surely nothing more unedifying then watching devotees batter unbelievers into submission in the name of the only true God! Because I happen to be one of those odd people who feels equally at home in a cathedral, synagogue, temple or mosque, I recognize the power inherent in all the major faiths and urgently desire to see that power harnessed for the welfare and good of humanity. Thus far, thank God, we have succeeded in Zambia in avoiding the undesirable alternatives: religious contention and strife on the one hand, and on the other the creation of some drab compromise which would lead to the loss of the distinctive character of this rich variety of faiths. There are many points of difference, even among the main religions represented in our country, which seem at this moment in history to be irreconcilable, but there ought surely to be common ground in a high view of Man as the paramount creation of the Supreme Being.

4 Song of Religiosity
Michel Kayoya

This poem, taken from the second book of the martyred
Burundi priest Michel Kayoya, strongly castigates those
African Christians whose religious faith is superficial and
irrelevant to the real needs of their country. So much
Christianity in Africa, he thinks, is an infantile religiosity.
An authentic African spirituality must help people make a
frontal attack on the causes of underdevelopment, not lull
them into the acceptance of an inhuman situation.

I see underdevelopment;
I see religiosity.
People sleep
With a false hope,
Formula of a faith not lived
In the space-time dimension
Of integral development —
Of the true Gospel.

I see underdevelopment;
I see religiosity,
Tranquil consciences,
Satisfied hearts.
Hey there!
How does it happen
That a brother is wounded?
                is naked?
Hey there!
A brother is blind,
            does not know how to read
            from the book
            of technological life.

I see underdevelopment;
I see religiosity;
I see superficial charity;
I see half-hearted charity;

I see alms-giving charity
A charity that is afraid
Of making a frontal attack
On the real causes of underdevelopment.
        I call religiosity
        your religion,
        your Sunday religion,
        your Sign-of-the-Cross religion,
        your religion of a seven-year old.

I see underdevelopment,
I see religiosity,
Adult human beings who do not know how to
        recognize the causes of misfortune.
I see the religiosity
Of educated people who cloak themselves with
   the right to go, humble and resigned, to
   kneel before the village magician.
I see religiosity . . .

Religiosity,
Instinctive stage, infantile stage,
Sunday cloak,
Borrowed cloak.

Religiosity,
Shrunken dress — gala frock
Kept hung up
On a rusty nail
In a locked cupboard
    for the rest of the week.

Religiosity,
Stale leaven,
Screeching engine
In need of lubrication.

Religiosity,
Tattered raincoat;
Varnish worn thin
By the inclement weather.

5 Love — the Essential Energy
Leopold Sédar Senghor

*Leopold Senghor is the poet-philosopher and President of
Senegal. Like Kayoya, and like the socialist philosophers
Mark and Engels, he urges the absolute necessity of material
development, of 'building the earth'. Unlike Marxist
socialism, Senghor's African Socialism is inspired by a
religious faith that preaches love. In this, he is strongly
influenced by the Jesuit anthropologist-theologian,
Teilhard de Chardin. The great evil of Marxism is its
inhuman militancy, its 'might is right' philosophy. The
African is a believer in God, and for him a Godless society is
a loveless society.*

God, as Super-Person, is a problem that all civilizations,
even socialism, have posed, for it is a vital necessity. In reality, what Marx and Engels criticize in the God of 'revealed
religions' is that he is posed 'as a final principle by an outer
impulse'. For Teilhard, it is precisely because the more
'man consciously forges his own history, the less it is influenced by unforeseen effects', that he turns to him for an
inner necessity, as Engels would say. Significantly, Engels
ended his introduction to *Dialectics of Nature* with a sentence that is already Teilhardian:'We have the certainty
. . . that (if matter) will exterminate its highest creation, the
thinking mind, it must somewhere else and at another time
again produce it.'

Thus, in the middle of this twentieth century, we are
pushed — or more exactly, drawn — toward that centre of
centres, that ultraconsciousness which is God. But once
again, this is merely the ultimate goal of our progress. Since
Marx, since the decline of capitalism and the emergence of
socialism, we have been at the threshold of the age of ultra-
reflection, which will lead us from well-being to maximum-
being before we are consummated in God. But first, we must
build the earth, our earth. For the African, for the Senegal-
ese, this need is all the more urgent, because we have not yet
even attained well-being. As one knows, our masses are still
prey to disease, poverty and ignorance.

Though it is true that the ultimate goal of man's generic activity is his realization as a god through love, we must find this love here and now, as we attain political, economic, social and cultural objectives. Both Berger and Teilhard have emphasized this point too much for us to pass it over in silence. European Marxists speak negatively about struggle, and positively about science, production, normative ethics, sometimes about art — and never about love. Nevertheless, if they have eliminated the love of God, they have not long been able to curb the love of men, which today once again wells up even in Russian poetry. As if 'socialist-realism' could ignore this human reality which Europe had deified! Referring to space research, Berger sees it as proof that 'men today are becoming gradually conscious of their *raison d'être*, which is to seek out one another, to meet one another and to unite'.

But it is Teilhard who proposes the most coherent theory concerning the nature and role of love in socialization, founded, as always, on the facts of experience. Starting from the law of complexification-consciousness, he shows us that progress in life is linked to 'centrity': to the union, centre to centre, of corpuscles and beings. For centres contain the maximum of psyche or spiritual energy. His second observation is that 'true union (or synthesis) does not confuse; it differentiates' by personalizing each component. ... What would be the use of human activity — political, economic, social, cultural revolutions — what would be the use of well-being if it did not lead to the maximum-being that we feel in love-union? Love for one's mate, one's family, one's fatherland or the planet Earth? Even politicians, to win the people's support in the midst of tension and international conflict, claim that peace is the goal of war. And they are not entirely wrong, since these tensions and conflicts only express the painful parturition of a new world of brotherhood, of love. Teilhard's socialization, our socialism, is nothing but the technical and spiritual organization of human society by the intelligence and the heart. After satisfying the animal needs and acquiring well-being by democracy and planning, men will then be able, in a union which is love, to realize their maximum-being. It is this love-union that we find as the focal centre of art, ethics and religion.

To explain, let us once again be guided by Teilhard. In the article 'Human Energy' that provides the title for Volume VI of his works, he affirms that love is the 'higher form of human energy'. Placing himself, like Marx and Engels, in the movement of history, he shows that 'universal love really represents itself to our experience as the superior phase of a transformation already begun in the mass of the Noosphere', as a general objective and final goal. Considered in this movement: Man totalizes his individual acts solely by love. Most often, he puts only a part of himself in his action. But if he considers the goal — human convergence with God — then, 'with the universe, in the least of his acts, he can establish total contact over the entire surface and in the depths of his being'. By totalizing our individual acts, love totalizes us at the same time — I mean that it personalizes us. This personalization, the synthesis of our faculties (intelligence and heart) and of our activities (thought and action) is also their symbiosis, for let us not forget that union differentiates. So it is that love for woman not only exalts each of man's faculties, but also makes of him a superior man, whether he be scientist, technician, or artist. 'If human love is so powerful,' Teilhard asks, 'how much greater the vibration when our beings encounter Omega?' Men are totalized, and socialized, in humanity solely by love. 'The passage from the individual to the collective is the crucial problem of human energy,' says Teilhard.

Although all the present political regimes — democracy, socialism, communism — have as their goal totalization and socialization without depersonalization, they fail in their attempt. This is because they sacrifice the part to the whole, the person to the collectivity. Since a materialist postulate underlies this, and since the collectivity is conceived solely as a technical organization, it does not attract; to push the individuals towards it, one must resort to constraint and violence. This is the reason for the failures. But if one conceives of the collectivity as human convergence cemented by liberty, equality, fraternity — terms that Marx scorned — and if one places the love of the Super-Person above human love, there will naturally be a powerful attraction to group individuals without constraint. For once again 'union differentiates', love personalizes.

I have often spoken of the role of the undeveloped nations in the building of the international community. Because the Negro Africans have kept a sense of brotherhood and dialogue, because they are inspired by religions that preach love, and above all because they live those religions, they can propose positive solutions for the construction of the international as well as the national community. The importance of love as essential energy, the stuff of life, is at the heart of Negritude, underlying the black man's ontology. Everywhere the couple — male-female — translates the integrality of the being. To be sure, procreation as the means of perpetuating the family and species occupies an important place in Negro-African society. But let us not be deceived: beyond the embrace of the bodies is the complementary union of souls.

6 Zero-Hour
Wandera-Chagenda

Senghor's picture of African Socialism is perhaps an ideal one. Contemporary Africa — with or without Marxist influence — is a violent continent. The younger generation is more sceptical and yet still basically searching and hopeful. Wandera-Chagenda was born in 1955 and comes from the Kenya-Uganda border area. He received most of his education in Uganda, but is a Kenyan. In this short poem he meditates on a reality that is already very much part of experience in the Africa he knows — death. Death is pitiless, like the fury of a Masai warrior stabbing his enemy. How helpful is the priest in making peace between the combatants? The poet is uncertain. Death is a zero, but it is still a countdown for something.

The giant finger
triggering death
lingers,
precariously
in the certainty
of those mumbled farewells . . .

a priest
to negotiate your peace?

Masai-warrior-fashion: enraged,
the arm of death
shoots sharp-spiked arrows,
to batter the pulsating
heart, violently;
as a gale strikes a weary ship;
silently crawling into
the immobility
of zero hour.

7 The End of All Seekings
Camara Laye

Still on the subject of death, Camara Laye, the Guinean writer, describes the end of his hero's quest in The Radiance of the King. *Clarence, the impoverished white traveller, felt the attraction of an African divine king. Conned, exploited and degraded in his own eyes and those of others, Clarence is physically and spiritually naked before the purity of the boy-king. Critics have suggested that the reader is intended to draw his own conclusions and discover his own meanings in this book. Whether or not there are any parallels in Islamic spirituality, the Christian thinks automatically of the repentant soul standing before God. One is reminded of Newman's* Dream of Gerontius *or George Herbert's* Love Bade Me Welcome.

'Is this the way one dies?' he whispered to himself.

Obviously it was — one entered a padded silence, a thickly-feathered silence; one light in a diffused radiance, a soft, strong radiance, a radiance. ... But where was this radiance coming from? Clarence got up and went to the right-hand window from which this radiance seemed to be streaming. And then. ...

He saw the king. He saw him sitting under the arcade at the Naba's side, he saw him sitting in all his glory. And then he knew where the extraordinary radiance was coming from.

It seemed that he had been waiting all his life for this moment. Now that he saw this longed-for scene, he did not know if it was real, or if it was some mirage, some hallucination, an image projected by his own eyes upon the courtyard wall; an image that had taken shape so long ago, and that had been conjured up so often that the eyes finally seem to see it, divorced from all reality.

No, the scene was real, enough. An endless procession of servants was bringing presents and casting them down at the king's feet. Yet the king's eye never once rested on these presents that were piling up in front of him; he was looking straight ahead; and perhaps he saw nothing. Perhaps his eyes, as in Dioki's cavern, were simply turned in upon himself; perhaps that look which he bent upon a distant point was a purely outward show, the result of a distracted and almost disdainful condescension or aimiability. ... What else could it have been? There was nothing upon which the king could rest his eyes in this ignoble country of the South. This condescension was already a great favour, whatever the secret scorn that lay behind it.

Behind the king, among his dancing pages, among that great crowd of people who in truth were the only ones who were saved, stood Nagoa and Noaga. Their eyes kept looking from Clarence to the king and back again. Their eyes seemed to be saying to Clarence:

'But what are you waiting for? Don't you see it's the time for the presents? Don't you see it's time to present yourself? Hurry up, Clarence! Don't let the moment slip by. Don't lose a second!'

Yes, that was the sort of things the boys were saying; but it must have been sheer effrontery urging them on to say these things. For the more Clarence looked at the king, the more he realized what courage, what audacity would be needed to go up to him.

And it was not just his nakedness, it was not just his vileness which prevented Clarence from going up to him; it was something else — many other things. It was the fragility — the fragility as well as the great strength of the king — the same adorable fragility, the same formidable strength that Clarence had observed on the esplanade; the same smile too, the same far-off smile which, like the look in his eyes, could be taken for disdain, and which really seemed to float round his lips rather than be an actual part of them. And probably his garments, too, so many other things that would have taken a lifetime to enumerate. But above all, so much purity, so much blazing purity. All these prevented Clarence from going up to him.

'Those are the things I am losing forever,' said Clarence.

And he had the feeling that all was lost. But had he not already lost everything? The boys could give him as many pregnant looks as they liked, he would not go near the royal presence; he had the measure of his own unworthiness. He would remain forever chained to the South, chained to the

Naba and to the harem, chained to everything he had so thoughtlessly abandoned himself to. Oh! If only he could have his life again! But can one ever go back and start again? His solitude seemed to him so heavy, it burdened him with such a great weight of sorrow that his heart seemed about to break.

'And yet ... my good will ...,' he thought. 'It's not true that I was lacking in goodwill. I was weak, no one has ever been as weak as I am; and at nights I was like a lustful beast. Yet, I did not enjoy my weakness. I did not love the beast that was inside me; I should have liked not to be that beast. No it's not true that I was lacking in goodwill.'

But what use was this goodwill? Clarence was about to curse it, curse it for its failure to help him. And the tears sprang to his eyes.

But at that very moment the king turned his head, turned it imperceptibly, and his glance fell upon Clarence. That look was neither cold nor hostile. That look ... Did it not seem to call to him?

'Alas, Lord, I have only my goodwill,' murmured Clarence, 'and it is very weak! But you cannot accept it. My goodwill condemns me: there is no virtue in it.' Still the king did not turn his eyes away. And his eyes ... in spite of everything, his eyes seemed to be calling. Then, suddenly, Clarence went up to him. He ought to have bumped into the outer wall, but as he approached it the wall melted away, the hut behind him melted away, and he walked on.

He went forward and he had no garment upon his nakedness. But the thought did not enter his head that he ought first of all to have put his *boubou* on; the king was looking at him, and nothing, nothing had any more meaning beside that look. It was so luminous a look, one in which there was so much sweetness that hope, a foolish hope, woke in Clarence's heart. Yes, hope now strove with fear within him, and hope was growing stronger than fear. And though the sense of his impurity seemed to be holding him back, at the same time Clarence was going forward. He went on with stumbling steps; he stumbled as he trod on the rich carpet; every moment it seemed as if his legs or the ground beneath him were going to disappear. But he kept moving forward, forward all the time, and his legs did not betray him, nor did the ground open up under him. And that look . . . That look still did not turn away from him. 'My Lord! My Lord!' Clarence kept whispering, 'is it true that you are calling me? Is it true that the odour which is upon me does not offend you and does not make you turn away in horror?"

And because that look still calmly rested upon him, because the call was still going out to him, he was pierced as if by a tongue of fire.

'Yes, no one is as base as I, as naked as I,' he thought, 'and you, Lord, are willing to rest your eyes upon me!' Or was it because of his very nakedness? . . . 'Because of your very nakedness!' the look seemed to say. 'That terrifying void that is within you and which opens to receive me; your hunger which calls to my hunger; your very baseness which did not exist until you gave it leave; and the great shame you feel. . . .

When he had come before the King, when he stood in the great radiance of the king, still ravaged by the tongue of fire, but alive still, and living only through the touch of that fire, Clarence fell upon his knees, for it seemed to him that he was finally at the end of his seeking, and at the end of all seekings.

But presumably he had still not come quite near enough; probably he was still too timid, for the king opened his arms to him. And as he opened his arms, his mantle fell away from him, and revealed his slender adolescent torso. On this torso, in the midnight of this slender body, there appeared at the centre, but not quite at the centre . . . a little to the right — there appeared a faint beating that was making the flesh tremble. It was this beating, this faintly-beating pulse which was calling! It was this fire that sent its tongue of flame into his limbs, and this radiance that blazed upon him. It was this love that enveloped him.

'Did you not know that I was waiting for you?' asked the king.

And Clarence placed his lips upon the faint and yet tremendous beating of that heart. Then the king slowly closed his arms around him, and his great mantle swept about him, and enveloped him forever.

Part Two
Readings in African Christian Spirituality

Second Commitment: Man and His Integral Development

8 Jesus Christ — Universal Brother
Harry Sawyerr

If, for the African, the world is a world of the spirit, it is also strongly anthropocentric. For the Christian, Jesus Christ is the glory and epitome of what it means to be human. The closer we draw to humanity in Africa (and anywhere else in the world) the clearer will be our vision of Christ, for the Spirit of Christ is already at work, irrespective of the formal efforts made by the churches. Harry Sawyerr, one of the first Protestant African theologians and for long Principal of one of Africa's oldest colleges — Fourah Bay College, Sierra Leone (founded in 1827) — advises the Christian teacher to lay emphasis on the humanity of Christ. Christ is not so much 'chief' for an African Christian, as 'elder brother', his own flesh and blood. The African will then make the discovery that Christ is 'that man in whom God lives'.

In the African situation the Incarnation should be so presented as to emphasize that Jesus Christ was the manifestation of God's love for man, God's share in human sufferings, God's victory over death and all disastrous influences which throng man's everyday experiences. In short, African Christians should be helped to realize that Jesus Christ was born as I was, grew up as I did, perhaps with all innocent mischief found in a growing boy and girl, and was later persecuted by his contemporaries because he was fully dedicated to the service of God. He therefore suffered death because of his unflinching loyalty to God. But God raised him from the dead because he was 'that man in whom God lived, and acted (and still does act) humanwise'. In this way, we could affirm our Lord's affinity to man as a basis for presenting the Church as 'the Great Family' of which Jesus Christ is the head.

Christian Africans will thus be able to find in the Church that unifying influence which transcends tribe and clan, and particularly the many divisive influences which national independence tends to engender. The Church, as the Body of Christ, represents the *primum ens* ('first being') from which all Christians take their origin, and so the tribal affiliations of Christians give way to the totality of the community of the Church, with Jesus as its first member.

This interpretation of the role of Jesus Christ as that of an elder brother seems to be more readily accepted, and certainly more salutary than Paul de Fueter's suggestion that Jesus Christ should be presented to African converts and enquirers as chief. Fueter says: 'We preach Christ who is the real chief, the king for Africa. He is the ruler who comes and in whose presence all is forgotten, with whom one is secure forever.' We would suggest that chiefship is particularly vulnerable as a description of Jesus Christ, because: (a) chiefs lost their pristine power and influence in the old days of colonial rule; in the new independent states their positions are, generally speaking, quite precarious. (b) Chiefship does not, *per se,* imply unquestioned supreme rule. It has never done. The chief is always answerable to his council of elders who in a measure determine his tenure of office. Absolute despotism was never tolerated. The despot either lost his life or was compelled to commit suicide; at best he was deposed. (c) The chiefs of African tribesmen have never been readily accessible to the ordinary man. Under normal circumstances chiefs must be approached through middlemen with official titles, e.g. the Okyeame among the Yoruba (Nigeria), Lavale (mouthpiece) among the Mende of Sierra Leone. Even gifts offered to the chief have to be presented through middlemen. At court, as among the Mende, they are the official spokesmen. Only when a suppliant approaches the chief, not in his judicial capacity, but as father-protector, is there direct access to him. (d) Again, chiefs generally live in a walled settlement and are therefore not exposed to the ordinary contact of their subjects. Thus, for example, in former times the Alafin of Oyo (Nigeria) went out on official circuits veiled, and the King of Dahomey (Benin) was never seen whilst having his meals. The Akan King (Ghana) made very few public appearances so that the evil wishes of his subjects might not injure his *kra* (life-soul) and so expose him to death.

We therefore suggest that chiefship is unsuited to the person of Christ. But to represent Jesus Christ as the first-born among many brethren who with him together form the

Church is in true keeping with African notions. For Christians an effort must be made to bring home the mystical relation between Christ and the Christian of which St. Paul speaks (Eph. 2:19ff). This mystical relation with Christ has many important implications which deserve a separate treatment. We may, however, isolate a few.

By it we are adopted into sonship with God, because, as St. Paul tells us, Jesus Christ was ordained by God to become the firt-born among many brethen. Christians are equally ordained to be conformed (i.e. shaped) to the likeness of Jesus Christ (cf. Rom. 8:29, 1 John 3:2). This is man's true destiny, the means of overcoming the deeply ingrained feeling of insecurity which creates acute social and psychological problems among even Christian Africans. The non-Christian African feels insecure and frustrated, but he has a ready-made formula for dealing with his difficulties, be they sudden death, or sterility or bad success. He presumes witchcraft or a spirit, cultic, ancestral or demonic, and performs the appropriate religious rites which restores his self-confidence, and all is well again. The various spirits are, however, attempts to establish concrete manifestations of deity. To the Christian this attitude is obviously idolatrous. The pagan, however, understands his situation and can deal appropriately, sometimes adequately, with the spirits and deities involved. For him there is a visible manifestation of the presence of the spirits near to hand in the form of a totem, an idol or the memory of the ancestors; he understands the rule of life they require, and the compensations they impose in cases of violation of that rule. He also knows that they have no pity, but can be propitiated. More so, he knows how to dodge them. When, however, he becomes a Christian and is faced with a situation which breeds insecurity, he can longer fall back on the old familiar ways of solving his problem, because he does not find available any concrete manifestations whose aid he can press into service. He may be willing to give up his pagan beliefs and so cultivate a genuine confidence in God. But an attitude of total surrender to God seems difficult to sustain after two generations. The answer to this problem is to be found, in our view, in the Christian doctrine of the Incarnation.

9 Christ Is Black
Chukwudum B. Okolo

For the African, Christ is a kinsman, a brother. The next, logical step is to say that he is black. Chukwudum Okolo speaks for the new breed of Black Theologians in South Africa. Theirs is a theology of liberation which grows out of an unjust socio-political situation. Christ is on the side of 'diminished man', of the oppressed African in a white dominated world. The white Christian fashions his Jesus, his God in his own image, thereby justifying in his own eyes his world-mastery. This image must be smashed. Nevertheless, the reader has to ask himself: Is Christ limited by the particular plight of the black man today? Should doctrines be rejected because of their abuse by white Christians? And what of Christ's witness of love and suffering?

Whether the diminished man is a black South African under the rule of force, police brutality, segregation and other unjust laws of white minority government, or a black American in the bondage of racism and poverty, or a Latin American whose economic vitality has systematically been drained by capitalistic exploitation, his central concern and point of departure is the experience of his own world. He is a Christian and a Revolutionary; the former because he received both natural life and the life of faith as man-in-the-world — a concrete human being; the latter because he has found that his world has now become a broken one, broken up by alien forces of greed and power. It is in this sense that we can understand the words of an African Poet, Noemia de Souza, 'And ask no more to know what I am. I am nothing but a lump of flesh in which, its cry swollen great with hope, the revolt of Africa has emerged.'

Far from being the product of sterile intellectualism or sophistry, liberation theology is born out of human experience and remains rooted in a sensitive concern for concrete individuals with concrete needs. This accounts for the fact that although many theologians of liberation pursue their themes in various directions, their points of departure and convergence have always been historical situations to man. Hence Basil Moore, a South African theologian, defines 'Black Theology' as 'a situational theology', and he also adds: 'And the situation is that of the black man in South Africa.'

Likewise, the great impetus that the Theology of Liberation received from Latin America is deeply rooted in the experience of anguish of the masses. The power of diplomacy witnessed in that part of the world has produced, in the words of Alves, not only 'an oppressed man, but an oppressed consciousness as well'. The direction which he has taken is thus the result of experience. Perhaps the foremost spokesman of Black Theology in America is James Cone. The black cause and black situation form the cornerstone of his theological quest. 'The very existence of Black Theology,' he writes, 'is dependent on its ability to relate itself to the human situation unique to oppressed men generally and black people particularly. If Black Theology fails to do this adequately, then the Black Community will, and should, destroy it.'

A fundamental perspective common to liberation theologians is therefore the 'cruciality' of their starting-points, namely, man's historical situation — indeed, a concrete man in a concrete world. This means that liberation theologians and Third World Christians generally, the type of Jesus and Gospel preached, faith professed, religion practised, etc., must relate to their world and their suffering situation. This is not to say that religious truths must be of exclusively human experience but that they should inclusively be it — indeed that should be their very point of departure.

The African liberation theologians (gradually emerging) uphold the same criterion of relevance in their acceptance of Christian faith and its sources. 'The sources are important and relevant,' Basil Moore writes, 'in so far as they are able to speak to us in our situation. Knowing the situation of blacks in South Africa, it is also important to know out of what sort of context the Biblical sources, for example, come.'

Moore speaks from South African experience but his insight rings true of African priests and bishops as a whole who have inherited and been trained in 'colonial' Christianity. It is is no small wonder that such clergymen who are officially designated to serve their people become more dominated by ideas, principles and all sorts of legislation from Rome, America and Europe than by the sufferings and undeserved predicament of the poor in their native land, largely because their formation and educational system are a betrayal to their world. These have geared them to aim at a Western ideal of Christianity and priestly training. This, no doubt, is a capital crisis in the African Church today.

It would certainly be a gross misinterpretation to think that an unconditional rejection of laws and ideas from Rome and Western nations is advocated here, but to take Western theories, principles and laws as the starting-point is, ultimately, to court alienation and irrelevance. Whether it is a question of Christianity in Africa, Latin America or in any other Third World nation, a definite break from Western, colonial Christianity and its mentality is called for.

Gutierrez calls this 'an epistemological break'. Bonino seeks for a type of religion that is 'beyond colonial and neo-colonial Christianity'. Among African and black American thinkers and writers such expressions as 'white man's God', 'white religion' and 'white church' are common. They point to the type of cultural break necessary for an emergence of authentic Christianity and its symbols. Perhaps, Cone is most direct on this point. He writes: 'Black Theology must realize that the white Jesus has no place in the black community, and it is our task to destroy him. We must replace him with the Black Messiah, as Albert Cleage would say, a Messiah who sees his existence as inseparable from black liberation and the destruction of white racism.'

The cultural revolt against Western Christianity by African liberation theologians (and other Third World theologians) and their emphasis that Christ ought to be and 'is black' show a perspective crucial to their thought, which is, that Christian religion and its symbols ought to reflect the suffering masses and their exploited condition. 'Christ is black' for he is not 'identified with the blacks, and stands amongst us as the Black Liberator of the blacks,' Basil Moore writes.

The rejection of 'white God', 'white Church', 'white

Jesus', etc., is ultimately the same reason for rejecting a colonial mentality, and economic power structures that have impoverished developing nations and created conditions of interminable conflict among the people. It is no secret that Africans and their counterparts in other developing nations regard Western Christianity as aiding, or being in close alliance with, white power structures that have enslaved them and their world. Consequently, when they denounce 'Western Christianity' or 'white Christ', it is because this is seen as tied up with the colonialism and neo-colonialism that have created ghastly realities of hunger, unemployment, repression, racism and violence in the Third World. 'The black man knows also what the white man's arrival has done to black society itself,' Moore writes, and this, for him, is the main reason why Black Theology needs to explore images of God which are not sickening reflections of the white man's power-mad authoritarianism. Whiteness and Christianity, for Cone, become opposites. This can easily become a universal tenet among the oppressed people to the extent that Western Christianity is affected by, and inseparable from, colonial culture and its alienating effects on the colonized.

10 You Have Marked Us for This Continent
A young Ghanaian

The problem of white discrimination against blacks in southern Africa and in other parts of the continent is the subject of this poem in a collection of prayers by anonymous young writers in Ghana. This is not only a problem of human rights, it is a problem of Christian good faith. If there are different churches, there are not different heavens for blacks and whites. God is not black or white, but he is 'greater than Europe and Africa' and he loves humankind. Yet, when all is said and done, it is the blacks who are at home in Africa.

O Lord, O Ruler of the world,
O Creator, O Father,
this prayer is for Africa.
For our brothers in the South,
for our brothers in the North.
You know
that the white brothers have made their black brothers
second-class people.
O Lord this hurts us so much.
We suffer from this.
You have given us a dark skin
so that we may better bear
your strong sun.
Why have our brothers done this to us?
They are not better than we,
and we are not better than they.
What comforts us is
that you always love most
those who suffer most.
We call ourselves Christians on both sides.
But we go to different churches,
as if there were also different heavens.
The white men
still have power in parts of Africa.

Help them to use their power wisely
and accept us as brothers.
Take the mistrust out of their hearts and minds
and make them share with us,
for this is our continent,
or, more truly, yours;
and you have marked us for this continent
and them for the North.
We also pray for ourselves.
O Lord,
keep our hearts free from hatred.
And let us also be grateful for what
missionaries have done here
and others too, for government and for the economy.
Let us become brothers again,
as it should be among your children.
You have died for all,
and risen,
Halleluja!
We praise you, our Father,
who are greater than Europe and Africa;
who love where we hate;
who long ago could have destroyed us.
But you love us so much
and we have not deserved it.
Praise be to you, O Lord!
Amen.

11 Authentic African Spirituality
Laurenti Magesa

*Racism is one of the ways in which humanity is 'diminished'
in Africa; poverty is another. Laurenti Magesa is a Roman
Catholic priest and theologian, born in 1946 in the Musoma
region of Tanzania. Having taught dogmatics at Kipalapala
Seminary, he is now doing further studies at Ottawa
University in Canada. Africa, thinks Magesa, calls for a
spirituality which is concerned with the glory of man. Our
encounter with God will take place first of all on the earth,
not in the skies. The African Christian must be strongly
committed to human development.*

In the African context the Spirit is definitely indicating that
it is certainly not right for the Church to be concerned only
with eternity in her proclamation of the Gospel. Life here is
important as an aspect of salvation, as many recent Church
documents attest. Sorely needed, therefore, is an authentic
Christian spiritual life relevant to present-day Africa. This
precludes the sort of spirituality which has no flesh and
blood, a zombie — or disincarnated spirituality. In a word,
Africa has no need of spiritualism. On the contrary, Africa is
crying for a Christian spirituality which has form, which is
incarnated; which acts and so offers tangible results in
terms, that is, of bringing about peace, justice and reconciliation among men just as Jesus came to do. Africa calls for a
spirituality which is concerned with the glory of man for, as
St. Irenaeus said, so many years ago, 'The glory of God is
man fully alive.' Christian spirituality in Africa must act in
the world for divine ends. It must be existential.

There is no other basis of Christian eschatalogical hope,
the eternal order, than the temporal order of people, work,
dust, painful contradictions but also of development; this
order of the passion, death but also resurrection of Jesus
Christ. Freedom from poverty, ignorance and disease; aspi-
ration for peace, justice and liberation from all sorts of dehumanizing conditions of life — these are the joys and hopes,
the griefs and anxieties of Africa.

The one effective witness of the Church's faith in God is

her tireless effort, not so much to lead people into the Church, as to proclaim the kingdom of God to all men primarily by commitment to the transformation of this world through social change, through helping man to become his best.

That is why Christian theology in Africa must take account of the fact that 'the earth is the Lord's and the fullness thereof' (Ps. 24:1), and avoid the error of looking for God only, or even primarily, in the skies. The whole world is full of him and theology must begin its investigations, its exploration into him here. The way for the Church in Africa to the most telling encounter with God is therefore commitment to the world. Theology must start with the horizontal plane, with people where they are and how they live.

12 Christian Commitment in Africa
John Zoa

*There are many obstacles in the path of a Christian
commitment to human development in Africa. John Zoa is
the dynamic Roman Catholic Archbishop of Yaoundé, the
capital of Cameroun, who made a memorable impact on the
Second Vatican Council, held at Rome in the first years of
his country's independence. Here, in the year after the
closing of that council, the Archbishop describes the
reluctance of Christians to involve themselves in the affairs
of the world. In the colonial era missionaries did the
Africans' thinking for them. Today they are disorientated
and critical of post-independence failures. But the onus is on
them to become involved and to get organized.*

The problem that faces us is the problem of a race that has
already been evangelized. The people of this race possess a
culture that was not understood by those who brought Revelation to them. This race came to know the Church during
an era of colonization when certain ways of acting were in
vogue. Today this race has bishops who received their formation during this era, but who nonetheless are able to experience in themselves the drama of their own people. Thus
they are questioning themselves not only concerning the
new world they want to become a part of, but also concerning the faith they have embraced. Do not get the idea that we
have doubts about our faith. Still, we have before our eyes,
inscribed in our very history, a question mark: 'How is our
faith to be integrated into the new and changed demands of
the contemporary world?' I am not familiar with all of
Africa. I speak particularly of Cameroun. Still, I am of the
opinion that by and large the situation in most countries of
Black Africa is not much different.

There are two merging factors. Before being evangelized
and coming into contact with the West, the people of Africa
possessed a genuine structure. Underlying this structure
was a philosophy of life that was never given explicit expression. Also underlying it was an attitude towards society. In
the case of south Cameroun the basic unit of society was the

clan or tribe: a more or less numerous group of people organized around an elder who constituted a link between the deceased and the living. This elder held in his hands political, diplomatic, economic and military power. He was also a priest. Thus, the clan was a closed group. We can even say it was a totalitarian group in which the individual gladly sacrificed himself for the existence and survival of the group. Its economy was what Europeans classify as a subsistence economy.

When we Africans came into contact with Europe, Africa was not asked what structure she wished to preserve. She was a colony. Certain laws were imposed upon her. Certain practices were established that she had to submit to. During this period the work of evangelization took place. There have been various views expressed concerning the methods used in evangelization and the motives for embracing the faith. Now, after sixty or seventy years, our country has become independent and we are faced with many problems.

The mission of the Church is to teach the law of charity in the situation we have described. It we were to say that it is our intention to give a description of the new dimensions of charity in Africa we would, no doubt, be obliged to outline the foundations on which these new dimensions can rest. Should they be based on the clan, or rather on the phenomenon of socialization which is found throughout the West and the whole world?

My opinion is that it is beyond doubt the African point of view that must govern our choices, our thinking and our decisions, and also decide what kind of religious education must be given to the people of Africa. The Church of Christ must strive in Africa to educate to Christian charity while at the same time heeding what already exists in Africa.

This charity must raise itself up to the level of the great solidarities of humanity. In its pedagogical orientations, however, it must take into account the basic orientations and avenues of approach to the soul of the African.

It is not then really surprising that we find among Christians today a sort of disorientation. When we speak to Christians about their responsibilities in the world and about assuming responsibility for the organization of the world, invariably, they are astonished and react as if the Church

were interfering in politics. There is a real problem here.
The formation of today's African bishops and African
priests pivoted on this same way of looking at things and
this sort of spirituality, so they have a hard task before them.
They have to make a truly spiritual and interior readjust-
ment and then give expression to this new state of mind in
their actions and in their efforts to educate the laity. If we
expect the Christian Church to assume the task of building
up the Africa we desire, Christians must acquire a true
understanding of what the lay state is. We are referring to
the involvement of Christians in building the cosmos and
travelling along the road to heaven through this involv-
ment.

We can notice a spirit of irresponsibility: this stems from
the education imparted in the clan and that given by the
colonial powers. When independence came, Africans took
over from white men, and people near the bottom of the lad-
der hoped that this change-over would immediately bring
about improvements. The immediate improvements anti-
cipated failed to materialize and even worse, in some cases
retrogression seems to have set in. The case of cocoa cultivated for export is an example of this. Co-operatives were
already in existence before the coming of independence and
were paying better prices than they are now after three years
of independence — though the producer had been promised
an increase in price. So ordinary Africans are both disillu-
sioned and dissatisfied. And it is these ordinary Africans
that constitute the masses that the Church is expected to
form and develop and help to equip for the building of a
new Africa.

Without a knowledge of this background it is impossible
to understand the role that falls to Christian endeavours in
the building of Africa. It is our obligation to form a laity capable of assuming responsibilities in the Africa to be con-
structed. But at the same time we find ourselves faced with
demands of an immediate nature which makes it impossible
for us to carry on the research needed in order to develop the
methods of education that are most suited to Africa.

Now you do understand our difficulties. Those of us who
are in continual and close contact with the people sense the
need for the people to participate in the exploitation and

development of the country. We can launch many activities in our parishes and in the lay apostolate, but we very quickly discover that a multitude of activities, though undertaken with the best of intentions, either accomplish nothing at all or are but short-lived. This happens because, though the efforts of Catholics and other Christians to organize the masses may be numerous, they cannot accomplish a great deal in the absence of an integrating plan, a plan that integrates efforts of a non-governmental nature.

There are not only economic aspects to the problem of development. There is also the psychological aspect. And in our opinion it is here that the Church has a special role to play. South Cameroun counts nearly 800,000 Catholics and almost 600,000 Protestants. So if the Christian churches could succeed in incorporating their interest in development into their catechesis and formation of the faithful, the role they play thereby could prove to be a decisive one. In actual practice how can the mission of the Church to evangelize, sanctify and educate consciences be reconciled with that of helping the faithful to take on the job of nation-building?

To our mind the traditional teaching of the Church on this point is clear enough. It is the unchanging task of the Church to carry out the mission entrusted to it by Christ: 'Go, teach, make disciples of all nations, baptize them in the name of the Father, the Son and the Holy Spirit, and teach them to keep the commandments.' It is therefore the unchanging mission of the Church in Africa and everywhere to announce the Truth through the Word of God, to sanctify men by means of the sacraments and the graces they impart and to form consciences. The Church in Africa has the same role as the Church in every country, namely to be the light of society and a leaven in it. However, in Africa and in all developing countries this role takes on exceptional importance. Why? Because events in Africa today are giving the Church the opportunity to take part in the birth of institutions and the establishment of economic structures that will determine the future of our countries.

So it is of capital importance for the Church in Africa to seek out ways of educating our faithful to focus their attention on these objectives. In Europe it is commonplace, when trying to predict the future of religion in Africa, to say that Africa is very religious. And this is true. Nonetheless, in my opinion religious belief in Africa is in grave jeopardy unless we make an effort in the direction of desacralization. Herein lies a paradox, for the African has always felt the realm of the sacred to be all encompassing. However, in the modern technological world, whose influence on our lives is constantly mounting, there is a danger that the African may cast aside his religious convictions in the process of revising his naive conceptions about what is sacred in his eyes. Hence it is for the defenders of the realm of the spirit in Africa, where Christians are in the front ranks, to be the first to assert the autonomy, the originality and even the religious nature of the profane.

13 Inertia
Wandera-Chagenda

Wandera-Chagenda, the poet from East Africa, deals with the problem of human development in his own way. Contemporary Africa is a Limbo, a kind of dream-world in which the African is not fully awake or alive. He is haunted by the persistent challenge to get up. Africa is in need of a resurrection.

In Limbo
Our weary bodies
Moan, wrestling in our dreams
With the impertinent question:
Why don't you resurrect your
Humanity?

14 The Christian Rebellion
Julius Nyerere

Julius Nyerere is probably the most respected statesman of Africa. As President of Tanzania, he has taught his people a philosophy of self-help, equal opportunity and co-operative living, the brand of African socialism known as ujamaa *(familyhood). In this address which he gave to American Roman Catholic missionary sisters in New York in 1970, he tackles Christian inertia in a forthright way. Christianity must not be an inward-looking religion. It must rebel against, not side with, the unjust structures of the world. It must help people take control of their lives.*

The purpose of development is man. It is the creation of conditions, both material and spiritual, which enable man the individual, and man the species, to become his best. That is easy for Christians to understand because Christianity demands that every man should aspire towards union with God through Christ. But although the Church — as a consequence of its concentration upon man — avoids the error of identifying development with new factories, increased output or greater national income statistics, experience shows that it all too often makes the opposite error. For the representatives of the Church and the Church's organizations frequently act as if man's development is a personal and 'internal' matter, which can be divorced from the society and the economy in which he lives and earns his daily bread. They preach resignation; very often they appear to accept as immutable the social, economic and political framework of the present day world. They seek to ameliorate intolerable conditions through acts of love and kindness as long as the beneficiary of this love and kindness remains an object. But when the victims of poverty and oppression begin to behave like men and try themselves to change those conditions, the representatives of the Church stand aside.

My purpose today is to suggest to you that the Church should accept that the development of peoples means rebellion. At a given and decisive point in history men decide to act against those conditions which restrict their freedom as

men. I am suggesting that, unless we participate actively in
the rebellion against those social structures and economic
organizations which condemn men to poverty, humiliation
and degradation, then the Church will become irrelevant to
man and the Christian religion will degenerate into a set of
superstitions accepted by the fearful. Unless the Church, in
its members and its organizations, expresses God's love for
man by involvement and leadership in constructive protest
against the present conditions of man, then it will become
identified with injustice and persecution. If this happens, it
will die — because it will serve no purpose comprehensible
to modern man.

For man lives in society. He becomes meaningful to himself and his fellows only as a member of that society. Therefore, to talk of the development of man, and to work for the
development of man, must mean the development also of
society, and of that kind of society which serves man, which
enhances his well-being and preserves his dignity. Thus the
development of peoples involves economic development,
social development and political development. And at this
time in history it must therefore imply a divine discontent
and a determination for change. For the present condition
of men must be unacceptable to all who think of an individual person as a unique creation of a living God. We say man
was created in the image of God. I refuse to imagine a God
who is poor, ignorant, superstitious, fearful, oppressed,
wretched — which is the lot of the majority of those created
in his own image. Men are creators of themselves and their
conditions, but under present conditions we are creatures,
not of God, but of our fellow men. . . .

The Church cannot uplift a man; it can only help him to
provide the conditions and the opportunity for him to co-
operate with his fellows to uplift himself. What does this
mean for those who give their lives to the service of the
Church?

Firstly, it means that kindness is not enough; piety is not
enough; and charity is not enough. The men who are now
suffering from poverty, whether they are in the Third World
or in the developed world, need to be helped to stretch themselves; they need to be given confidence in their own ability
to take control of their own lives. And they need to be helped

to take this control, and use it themselves for their own pur-
poses. They need their *uhuru*, and meaningful *uhuru*. This
is important to the Church, as well as to mankind. For until
men are in a position to make effective choices, few of them
can become Christians in anything but name. Their membership of the Church will be simply another method by
which they seek to escape from a consciousness of their misery: if you like, religion becomes a kind of opium of the
people.

Everything, therefore, which prevents a man from living in
dignity and decency must be under attack from the Church
and its workers. For there is nothing saintly in imposed
poverty and, although saints may be found in slums, we cannot preserve slums in order to make them breeeding
grounds for saints. A man who has been demoralized by the
conditions under which he is forced to live is no use to himself, to his family or to his nation. Whether he can be of
much use to God is not for me to judge.

The Church has to help men rebel against their slums; it
has to help them to do this in the most effective way it can be
done. But most of all the Church must be obviously and
openly fighting all those institutions and power groups
which contribute to the existence and maintenance of the
physical and spiritual slums — regardless of the consequences to itself or its members. And, wherever and however
circumstances make it possible, the Church must work with
the people in the positive tasks of building a future based on
social justice. It must participate actively in initiating, secur-
ing and creating the changes which are necessary and which
will inevitably take place.

Only by doing this can the Church hope to reduce hatred
and promote its doctrine of love to all men. Its love must be
expressed in action against evil and for good. For if the
Church acquiesces in established evils, it is identifying itself
and the Christian religion with injustice by its continuing
presence.

Secondly, the members of the Church must work with the
people ... it is important that we should stress the working
with, not the working for. For it is not the task of religious
leaders to try to tell people what they should do. What is
necessary is sharing on the basis of equality and common

humanity. Only by sharing work, hardships, knowledge, persecution and progress, can the Church contribute to our growth. And this means sharing in every sense as 'members of one another'. For if the Church is not part of our poverty, and not part of our struggle against poverty and injustice, then it is not part of us.

I think another changing function of religious members is in relation to the social services. In many areas of the world — and particularly in Africa — the Catholic Church has built its own schools and hospitals. These have been invaluable; they have provided education and medical care when there would otherwise have been none. But I believe that such provision should be an interim measure, and that, wherever possible, the Church members should be working with, and through, the organizations owned and controlled by the people themselves. Nuns and Brothers should be working in State Schools and nursing in State Hospitals; they should be District Nurses in a national, regional or city structure. By adopting this kind of policy wherever it is possible, the Church will be showing that its purpose is service to the people, and not control of them. By separating the provision of service from its evangelical activities, the Church will make clear that it desires men's conversion to Christianity to come from conviction, not from gratitude or from the compulsion of indebtedness.

Finally, I believe that members of religious organizations must encourage and help the people to co-operate together in whatever action is necessary for their development. What this will mean in practice will vary from one country to another, and from one part of a country to another part. Sometimes it will mean helping the people to form and run their own co-operative villages. Sometimes it will mean helping the people to form their own trade unions — and not Catholic trade unions, but trade unions of workers regardless of religion. Sometimes it will mean the Church leaders involving themselves in nationalistic freedom movements and being part of those movements. Sometimes it will mean co-operating with local Governments or other authorities; sometimes it will mean working in opposition to established authorities and powers. Always it means the Church being on the side of social justice and helping men to live together and work together for their common good. ...

It is not necessary to agree with everything a man believes or says in order to work with him on particular projects or in particular areas of activity. The Church must stand up for what it believes to be right; that is its justification and purpose. But it should welcome all who stand on the same side and continue regardless of which individuals or groups it is then opposing.

A good does not become evil if a communist says it is a good; an evil does not become good if a fascist supports it. Exploiting the poor does not become a right thing to do because communists call it a wrong thing; production for profit rather than meeting human needs does not become more just because communists say it leads to injustice. Organizing the society in such a manner that people live together and work together for their common good does not become an evil because it is called socialism. A system based on greed and selfishness does not become good because it is labelled free enterprise. Let the Church choose for itself what is right and what is wrong in accordance with Christian principles, and let it not be affected by what other groups or individuals do or say. But let it welcome co-operation from all those who agree with its judgements. ...

We know that we are fallible men and that our task is to serve, not to judge. Yet we accept into the Church (provided only that they come to Mass every Sunday and pay their dues or contribute to missionary activities) those who create and maintain the present political and economic system. But it is this system which has led to millions being hungry, thirsty and naked; it is this system which condemns millions to preventable sickness, and which makes prisoners of men who have the courage to protest. What right, then, have we to reject those who serve mankind, simply because they refuse to acknowledge the leadership of the Church, or refuse to acknowledge the divinity of Jesus or the existence of God? What right have we to presume that God Almighty takes no notice of those who give dedicated services to those millions of his children who hunger and thirst after justice, just because they do not do it in his name? If God were to ask the wretched of the earth who are their friends, are we so sure that we know their answer? And is that answer irrelevant to those who seek to serve God? . . .

Yet this is not all. Just as we must not be afraid of working with men of different religious convictions or of none, so too we must not allow ourselves to be frightened by new ideas, new plans, or new projects. The world needs new ideas, new organizations as much as it needs to apply the truths of Christianity; indeed we need new ways of applying these truths in the technological world of the twentieth century. It is the job of the Church to find these new paths forward, and to recognize them when they are pointed out by others. Fear of the future, and of the needs of the future, is no part of Christianity. Ours is a Living Faith: if you like, a Revolutionary Faith, for faith without action is sterile and action without faith is meaningless.

'I am come that they may have life and may have it more abundantly.' What all this amounts to is a call to the Church to recognize the need for social revolution, and to play a leading role in it. For it is a fact of history that almost all the successful social revolutions which have taken place in the world have been led by people who were themselves beneficiaries under the system they sought to replace. Time and again members of the privileged classes have joined, and often led, the poor or oppressed in their revolts against injustice. The same thing must happen now.

Within the rich countries of the world the beneficiaries of educational opportunity, of good health, and of security, must be prepared to stand up and demand justice for those who have up to now been denied those things. Where the poor have already begun to demand a just society, at least some members of the privileged classes must help them and encourage them. Where they have not begun to do so, it is the responsibility of those who have had greater opportunities for development to arouse the poor out of their poverty-induced apathy. And I am saying that Christians should be prominent among those who do this, and that the Church should seek to increase the numbers and the power of those who refuse to acquiesce in established injustices. . . .

Friends: there was a time when the Christian Church was persecuted and its members held in contempt and derision. Are the societies in which the Catholic Church now operates so just, or so organized for the service of God and Man, that it is unnecessary to risk a similar rejection in the pursuit of social justice? I do not believe so. I believe with Teilhard de Chardin that: 'A Christian can joyfully suffer persecution in order that the world may grow greater. He can no longer accept death on the charge that he is blocking mankind's road.'

15 A Struggle That Is Human
Michel Kayoya

Michel Kayoya, the Roman Catholic priest who gave his life in 1972 because of his outspoken criticism of the authorities in Burundi, returns to the theme of discrimination. This time it is not the discrimination of white against black, but the 'more terrible colonization' of brother by brother. Development does not mean aping a Capitalist or Communist West. Both these systems encourage a dehumanizing violence. Africa must return to its own authentic values, its own human qualities, renewed within Christianity.

It is not by raising Africa to the level of the West that we Africans can answer the world's invitation.

It is not by endowing Africa with every material good that we shall grow.

It is not by integrating Africa into world commerce that we shall hand over to the world what Destiny asks of us.

Certainly Africa must be modernized, and as quickly as possible Africa must be enriched. We must work for that with all our strength, not with any ambition to equal or compete with the West, but so that these goods may be a cloak to cover us as we go forward to build up a renewed humanism.

This cloak must cover our own hearts
Our conception of *ubuntu* (human qualities)
Our love of *ubuvyeyi* (parental dignity)
Our practice of *ubufasoni* (nobility of origin)
Our sense of *ubutungane* (integrity)
The respect for Imana (God) — our father's legacy to us.

Let us throw ourselves into such a commitment
There is no time to lose
But do not let us forget
Like everything that burgeons, man too needs bounds
The wild fruit tree is the one with neither garden nor gardener
Its fruits degenerate

Become progressively wilder
Our commitment must remain within bounds.

After one colonization, were we going to be subjected to
another?
Another more terrible colonization?
A colonization by the meanness which every heart con-
ceals Laziness and pride
Burdens that weight on the heart of man and prevent him
from growing
The struggle for liberation becomes a struggle between
brothers tearing each other apart.

When I heard people preaching progress towards unity
I used to feel a real joy
A single people
One heart
One humanity
It is fine when man pays attention to it and submits to it
It is wonderful to see all that brings men together!
Man is not made free by force
Brutal force
Pressure
Brute force stupifies
A human combat is one that touches the heart of man and
leads him to become freer in himself
Brute force leads to dehumanization
The man who uses brute force believes he is alone
The man who believes he is alone cannot perfect himself
Each segregation
Contributes to the worst segregation of all
The segregation of brothers within the heart of the same
family.

Where is the man who knows himself as both little and
great?
Where is the man who becomes more of a man by taking
account of respect?
Where is the man who draws closer to the Infinite by casting a human glance at all his equals?
When I heard them speak of a free man

Of man exercising all his manly attributes
In the real sense
Of beauty
Of Good
I was satisfied
Provided that we did not forget that the true
The beautiful
The good
Are not only a human creation.

Capitalism deceived me
Communism spied on me in my surging towards
humanism
I wanted Africa to contribute to human values of relation-
ship
Of dependence
Of hospitality
Of the heart
Of a hierarchy of self knowledge
Of metaphysics
Of mystery
Of joy
Of human sadness.
I wanted my people to find strength to let their children
keep the superhuman value of their rights
To live by dancing their optimism about existence
To keep their communion in the happiness and misery of
their neighbour.

I wanted my people to reject the Communist Patrimony
as they would reject poison.
I wanted my people to turn their backs on egoistic Capitalism to adopt a vital attitude in a social personalism where
individualism and ultra-liberalism would be diminished.

I wanted my people's children to have a true philosophy
Their ancient philosophy renewed.

16 Prevention of Cruelty to Human Beings
Henry Okullu

Henry Okullu is the Anglican Bishop of Maseno South in western Kenya. Besides his present ministry in Kenya, he also has experience of conditions of life in neighbouring Uganda where he worked for many years. He is one of the most outspoken churchmen in Africa today, fearlessly condemning the infringement of human rights both under the regime of Idi Amin and even in his own country. In this short, but typical, passage he is referring to the tribal war in Burundi, the conflict in which Michel Kayoya died. It is a passage that can stand for his numerous, subsequent statements on the same topic that refer to other countries of Africa.

In Africa the Society for the Prevention of Cruelty to Animals should be changed and instead be called the Society for the Prevention of Cruelty to Human Beings, since the latter's position is more precarious than that of animals. In the history of independent Africa, there has never been such a large-scale killing of animals in the way human life is repeatedly wasted in various parts of the continent. Not even in Kenya's Tsavo National Park where nearly 5,000 elephants died in 1972 through drought, can the situation be compared to a large-scale massacre of . . . men, women and children in a tribal war. . . .

Taking of human life is tragically becoming commonplace in Africa where large massacres occur with every turn of the year. The sanctity of human life is gradually becoming replaced by the idea that every man and woman is expendable at any time, if he is a thief, a hijacker or a political foe. The worst part, so far as Africa is concerned, is the wastage of life and human resources in civil wars. . . .

We as Christians can never believe that because a nation is made up of different ethnic groups it is impossible to live happily without animosity. The fault, therefore, perhaps lies with the leaders. Of all the great leaders in Africa, not a single one of them is above tribalism, in our opinion. If a leader came out in word and deed against the evil thinking that certain tribes are nobler than the rest, he would definitely be unpopular, but even if he ruled for only a limited period of time, history would never forget him.

Jesus Christ was in public life for only three years and then he was eliminated by the enemies of truth and justice, but what an impact he made! Jesus Christ lived and died for our freedom and its benefits are now enjoyed by people of all nations who avail themselves of those benefits. Jesus was a Jew, but the fruits of his death are not restricted to his fellow tribesmen alone. Let all African leaders follow the example of Jesus Christ! Let the evil of tribal governments be uprooted from the soil of Africa and the civil wars be minimized. It is only then that we can criticize South Africa's or Rhodesia's racist leaders in good conscience. For, essentially, racism and tribalism are the same thing, and the net result of practising them is the same — violence.

17 Martyrdom
Wandera-Chagenda

*Readers of this moving poem from East Africa will probably
have Uganda in mind — Uganda, the land of martyrs.
Wandera-Chagenda, speaking for the youth of Africa, asks:
Can we afford the luxury of 'unscheduled martyrs'? Africa is
bleeding to death from self-inflicted wounds. Skilled and
talented people are being annihilated faster than they can be
replaced. This is only 'a little protest' — but the slaughter
goes on. Africans point the guns at one another. Westerners
place the guns in their hands.*

This modern sacrifice
Reminds one of
The biblical lamb offering.
A life,
Even the life of a fly
Is an expensive sacrifice.
So, in our primitive airs,
Littlest knowledge of a
Utopia,
Let us not manufacture
Martyrs,
Unscheduled martyrs of our own
Kind. Allow us a little
Protest to assert our littleness . . .
But, alas, in toppling over
This black precipice,
Our stifled moans
Must sound more agonized
Than the menacing ecstatic howls
Of the Cobra's blood-dance!

18 Christianity as a Unifying Factor in a Developing Country
J. Akin Omoyajowo

Dr. Akin Omoyajowo lectures in the Department of Religious Studies of the University of Ibadan, Nigeria. He is also one of the leading Black Theologians in contemporary Africa. In this extract he sketches the havoc that has followed the ending of the colonial period. Colonization precipitated a social disintegration, leaving the people in the hands of black exploiters. The churches, by their scandalous disunity, contributed to the confusion. Marxism is not the answer. It is only a united Church that can be a principle of integral development and unification.

The developing nation is the nation which has just emerged or is emerging from the shackles of colonialism, whose human and material resources have been exploited or largely left undeveloped and which, in consequence, is faced with serious and urgent economic, social, technological and perhaps political problems. In such a developing nation the basic needs are obvious: food, clothing, shelter, security and a sense of dignity. The evils of colonialism in Africa are colossal. African institutions were broken by slavery and colonialism, while foreign cultures were thrust deeply into the very being of Africans. Integral development, however, must be regarded as essential in any developing nation. This means the comprehensive uplift of the whole community in all its many wants and needs on to a recognizably higher and better plane than before. . . .

This task is not an easy one. In some cases, situations created during the colonial days make the task almost impossible — especially in Africa. Attempts at industrialization and urbanization, with their accompanying detribalization have, to a large extent, disintegrated African family and social life. Consequently, religious and other values and sanctions of tribal life have broken up. . . . The secularization of life and conduct in an essentially religious society . . . and the havoc which the products of Western civilization played in the spiritual, religious and moral lives of Africans cannot be overstressed. In this age, therefore, of development the spiritual risks are very great. For, as we separate everyday life from religion, we are breaking up the unity and wholeness of life.

As the nations aspire towards integral development, we find extremes of human happiness and cultural development. Urban dwellers have an abundance of the amenities that the Government can provide — hospitals, transport, housing, security forces and other social services. In the rural areas these are completely absent. Even in the cities we always have . . . the 'problem of two worlds' — a heaven for the high class and a hell for the unfortunate. Unless the widening gap between the rich and poor is arrested, and if possible reversed, the very peace and stability of any society will be seriously jeopardized.

Also common in Africa is the appearance of local political schemers and 'economic gluttons' who have replaced the colonial exploiters. Instead of an honest sharing of equitable opportunities for everyone's self-fulfilment and self-realization, these local leaders in politics, business, education, etc., try very often to take the shortest route to acquire for themselves the maximum personal gain, prestige, immense wealth, however dirtily acquired, and they become oppressive, totalitarian and anti-Christian in their behaviour. . . .

These factors have continued to create situations of unrest, instability and disintegration in the developing nations. If the leadership is corrupted, whither does it lead the masses? If the gap between rich and poor continues to widen, and if the urban dwellers continue to live in prosperity while the inhabitants of the rural areas continue to live in poverty, how can we talk of unity, peace and social justice? These can be no meaningful integral development where the leadership is corrupted, immoral and pretentious. Such leadership will be tantamount to theft. The familiar occurrence of crime and corruption, especially in the political arena, the distorted direction of the industrial system because of an excessive stress on profit, the return to pre-Christian paganism in the name of cultural revival, the externalization of values because of radio and television, the generation-gap, the property-poverty-gap, drug-addiction and other terrible situations which have become the phenomena of our age, these are characteristic of the world that we inherit from a humanism which has proclaimed reason and rationality as the path to genuine humanity.

The question now is: Where does Christianity come in? What is the concern of Christianity in all this? Christianity cannot afford to think that the great human society for which Christ died should be abandoned to the powers of evil. Christ loves us and expects us to love humanity and to seek to save it as he did. . . . The alleviation of human suffering and the achievement of an abundant life for all have a primary claim in Christianity. Christianity must then work energetically toward the elimination of the social causes of suffering, and, at the same time, care for the victims of social injustice and misfortune as well. This concern for just relationships in society is one aspect of the compassionate ministry of Christ. . . .

The aim of the Church is to make of the individual a member of Christ and an heir of the Kingdom of God. But it does not seem that the Church has yet arrived at an answer to the question: What must we do to redeem society and mankind? And so it is unable to present itself as a unifying factor in a developing country.

In its present form Christianity does not seem to be properly equipped to face the challenge. It seems not to be interested in the integration of society, for although its proclamation is about one Lord, one faith and one Baptism, it is hopelessly and depressingly fragmented into a hundred diverse and often opposing directions. . . . The Church that will help to integrate a developing nation cannot identify itself with a particular social class, prefer a particular political philosophy or party. The Church which gives room for Christians to adjust the spirit of the Gospel to humanistic thinking and practice calls for urgent examination. Every denomination these days expresses a heresy. . . . Before we can address ourselves to the developing nations, we have to examine the sickness, the cancer that destroys a wholehearted commitment to the Lord of our lives.

All the same, the situation of society as an integrated whole, and as a community, cannot be abandoned to Marxism or to a recrudescence of our old religions in the guise of cultural revival. Admittedly humanism does provide an alternative spiritual direction right in the centre of Christendom. It has already conquered the West and it is now stepping into the developing nations.

However Christians have the responsibility to come forward and translate socialism in the light of Christian principles and, here in Africa, of African culture. If we want that unity and wholeness, the ownership and management of large-scale means of production must be vested not in individuals but in the people as a whole. Then there will be a national adoration of the true God, the source of everything, not the amassing by individuals of incalculable wealth whereby they hold men and families perpetually enslaved to them.

Christians are conscious of being heirs of God's manifold blessings and grace in Christ. This is why we believe that, although we belong to the Church, the Church belongs to the world which God loves. . . .

Part Two
Readings in African Christian Spirituality

Third Commitment: Culture and Community

19 The Challenge of Africanizing the Church
Dominic Mwasaru

The Church must take African culture seriously; this is a message that is being proclaimed by African Christians with increasing frequency and clarity. This means not merely an Africanization of personnel or even of forms of worship, but the adoption of new structures suited to the African way of life. Dominic Mwasaru is a young Roman Catholic priest from Eastern Kenya who sees this clearly. The following passage is taken from his prize-winning prose-poem published in 1974.

'What is this thing they call Christianity?
Sheer colonialism! Cultural suppression!
Sons of Africa, listen! Listen carefully!
The white man came with a book he called Bible.
His brother came after him with a staff of power.
They conspired together how to chain the African.
They pretended to make friendship with us,
We trusted them, we made pacts of friendship.
But you all know how this friendship was betrayed.
They turned against us with their superior weaponry,
They subjected us to their rule.
Our fathers supplied cheap labour for them;
Their very blood was sucked to feed the white man's family.
However, brothers, do not worry,
The staff-holder is routed.
Yes, he is still in southern Africa;
But even there he must go.
We cannot, nevertheless, rejoice;
Full victory is not yet achieved.
The Bible-bearer should also go.
Until he goes, our victory is incomplete.
We must be careful, though;
The Bible-bearer is cleverer than the staff-holder.
See how he has tamed some of our brothers!

They follow him like his dogs.
But we shall conquer.
Sons of Africa unite!
Shake off the shackles of political colonialism!
Cast off the chains of cultural colonialism!
Blessed be our ancestors!
Blessed be our heroes!'

Did you hear that?
Those are the heralds of death.
They are foretelling the death of the Church in Africa.
Did you recognize any of those voices?
Yes.
One was from the University of Accra;
Another from the University of Dar-es-Salaam;
And another from the University of Nairobi.
I think I also heard the voice of Okot p'Bitek.
He is a faithful son of Africa.
He is among the champions of African authenticity.
Why do they brand Christianity along with colonialism?
It seems they do not know what Christianity really is.
Most of the accusations arise from ignorance;
The accusers fail to distinguish cultural accidents from
the Essence of Christianity;
So they make sweeping statements.
Another reason may be reaction to the colonial era.
Past memories sometimes taste extremely bitter.
One is even tempted to spit out the 'whole thing'.
So, out of utter bias, they hurl unfounded accusations.
Let us ask the question again:
Why do they brand Christianity along with colonialism?
Is it just a question of ignorance?
Is it purely a matter of exaggerated patriotism?
Can their claims be refuted so easily?
No, I do not think so;
Their claims go beyond mere reaction.
They are questioning our 'docile' acceptance of foreign
structures.
They are asking why we should mimic the structures of
western churches.

Let us open our eyes to the signs of our times.
We cannot afford to shut our ears to these voices.
Yes, some are confused;
But some challenge the very depths of our hearts.
This is the time to heed the voice of prophets,
The voice of prophets within the fold;
And even of those outside the community of the chosen people.
Refusal to obey will only mean doom.
The structural revolution must happen;
Otherwise, the Church in Africa will gradually wither off.

20 The Theological Value of African Tradition
Charles Nyamiti

African culture is also a tradition, but a living tradition. This does not mean an interest in the past for the past's sake. Today there is a conscious recovery of a neo-African culture by the intelligentsia. African tradition is becoming a source and inspiration for new beginnings. This is the message of Dr. Charles Nyamiti, lecturer in Dogmatic Theology at the Roman Catholic Seminary of Kipalapala in Tanzania. He is the author of several works on the nature, scope and content of African Christian Theology. This passage is taken from his second book, The Scope of African Theology *published in 1973.*

Care should be taken not to judge too quickly that a given cultural phenomenon is incompatible with technical civilization, or that a socio-economic change will inevitably lead to the suppression of some existing African values. This is often maintained with reference to Western societies, which once possessed such values but lost them with the coming of industrialization. Such an argument is not cogent. The question is whether or not the West could have preserved such values in spite of industrialization. It does not necessarily follow that where the West has failed others should fail too. One should also remember that the actual Western societies contain not only cultural values useful to all men, but also deviations and loss of cultural goods which Africa still possesses. Hence, a cultural element is not necessarily to be despised as 'primitive' because Westerners no longer have it. Accordingly, a good working principle should be that no African cultural element should be rejected unless it can be proved that it is altogether incompatible with the modern African way of life.

One can already see from the foregoing the mistake of those who reject totally the past and fix their attention exclusively on the present and future of the African cultures. Their argument for the futility of the African past would be pertinent if adaptation based on traditional elements would inevitably lead to the adoption of archaic forms unfit for modern societies. But this, as we have seen, is not necessarily the case. Besides, how could one properly understand the present societies if one were to neglect their historical past? As J.V. Taylor so rightly points out, the African traditional world-view is continually reflected in the thoughts and attitude of Christian Africans; and one has 'to reckon seriously with the conscious recovery of a neo-African culture by the intelligentsia and their considered rejection of Western systems of thought and evaluation'. Add to this the fact that the African élite are a very small minority in the African communities. Most Africans are still leading a traditional way of life, and we have no guarantee that this state of affairs is going to undergo vast revolutionary changes in a few years to come. Are we going to base our theology exclusively on the mentality of a minority and neglect the masses? Is this lack of due pastoral concern not one of the reasons why modern theologians are doing so much harm to so many by representing a theology adapted to the élite but indigestible to the masses? Nor are the aspirations of the modern African youth sure signs of the ideals Africa has to pursue. It is in fact not always easy to tell whether such aspirations are genuine 'signs of the time' or the result of colonial deformation, or even of psychological immaturity.

Surely our earnest protest should be raised against ideas and methods which lead to the neglect of that immense and original cultural wealth prepared for centuries by the African genius and thereby leave the African almost culturally empty-handed. The history of Western cultures is characterized by various 'revivals', 'renaissances' and 'neo-s' of their past; and Africa would gain by following a similar course.

As to those who maintain that African traditional cultures are doomed to disappear in the face of the coming universal human culture, I would first point out that this view is contradicted by the facts. To give but one example: the French bishops, after having recently made a scientific investigation into the present societies, have come to the conclusion that 'the differences are more numerous in spite of the proximities and interdependencies; economies, cultures, ideologies, races, degree of development create distances more than proximities'.

What is perhaps even more important is that the
uniformization of cultures would be a great evil for humanity. It would bring about cultural impoverishment and its
evil consequences. The understanding of reality itself —
especially religious reality — would be pitifully weakened.
Each cultural system is timely and geographically limited,
and as such can better appreciate and express the aspects of
reality in keeping with it.

21 Roots
Wandera-Chagenda

'Roots' is a popular and emotive word among Blacks everywhere today, and Wandera-Chagenda, the poet from East Africa who speaks for African youth, has made it the title of this poem written specially for this anthology. Like Nyamiti, Chagenda sees the traditions of the African as a point of departure for invention and creativity. Africans have no wish to be passive consumers of Western cultural goods, the goods intended to replace what colonialism has destroyed. Discovering one's roots means discovering one's identity, recovering one's self-respect, taking control of one's own life.

Who are you
Charcoal-black man?
They ask.

I am one
Whose spirit you have exiled
Still, and hold in bondage,
One whose gods you have outlawed!

You shamed me
Duped me, brought me
Face to face with fear,
Ramming down my throat
Your civilization.

For centuries my spirit dwelt
In undisturbed repose.
The sanctuary
Of my homestead
Was protected jealously
By warrior-ghosts
Who in the nearby oak tree
Half-slept out the day.

Until *you* came

Unprompted
Uninvited
Bent on sheer destruction.

I am not
A mere consumer of your culture,
But I want to build
And to create
And to invent.
I need my roots
I need a firm foundation,
Point of swift departure.

Endlessly, I travel in pursuit
Of fleeing shadows,
But I will not yield
To your manipulation.
In this changing world
I need my own traditions.
These are they
That make me who I am.
Can *you* tell me who I am?

22 African Culture and Spontaneous Prayer
Laurenti Magesa

Fr. Laurenti Magesa, a Theology Lecturer from a Roman Catholic Seminary in Tanzania, identifies one important area for Africanization — the Christian liturgy. Public worship is the 'shop-window' of the Church, and if it appears foreign, the Church itself is judged to be foreign. If Christian worship in Africa is to conform to African culture, it must take account of the traditional spontaneity which characterizes African prayer. In any case, argues Fr. Magesa, this form of prayer brings the Church nearer to the actual life-situation of African Christians.

It is unfortunate that the perfect prayer has for a long time been considered to be the stereotyped, memorized or read kind, fitting all circumstances. The spontaneous type of prayer, directed by the Spirit, responding to particular human needs and feelings has almost totally been disregarded (by Catholics). Usually, particular needs and feelings are not met in official prayer formulas, so that these feelings continue to nag one with a queer sense of dissatisfaction. This is because stereotyped prayer does not usually respond to concrete life-situations. The idiom used cannot be easily understood, and, even if it is, it bears no relevance to the here and now popular or personal needs, and it takes no account of individual or group emotions and feelings. Emotions and feelings are very important elements in prayer as it is understood by the African and they determine the depth, the sincerity, even the worth of the prayer, not to say the wording and the mood. Such prayer can only be spontaneous.

Set forms of prayer or prayer formulas were very rare in Africa. African prayer was what may be termed 'charismatic improvisation' prompted by the needs of the hour. They were never stylized, but flowed spontaneously from the innermost depths of the heart, expressing emotions and feelings in clear idiom. Meaningfulness and the human quality of the prayer were prized above all else.

In stressing the importance of spontaneous prayer, I may give the impression that I am militating against the efficacy of so-called official prayer-formulas. However, if I am unduly underlining the value of spontaneous prayer, it is because the formalized prayer has had more than its fair share of emphasis at the expense of the former in the course of recent Church history. My own view is that we should take the middle roàd — pray spontaneously when occasion offers, especially among primary communities, such as the family, and use the official prayer forms as a basis for personalized prayer at gatherings of secondary groups like Sunday gatherings, where instantaneous prayer is hardly possible at first, because of the group's lesser sense of belonging and its varying needs. Since, sociologically, good organization in primary groups is a help to the individual members of that group to relate favourably to secondary groups, frequent spontaneous prayer by the primary groups will help the individuals, at least psychologically, to accommodate themselves to official prayer forumulas at the level of the largest secondary community, the universal Church.

For all their shortcomings, official prayer-forms certainly have their place in the African Church and I do not want to undermine them. For one thing, they have had the scrutiny of the highest, competent authorities in the Church and could easily be made stepping-stones to personal prayer. For another, they remind the Christian in a somewhat minor way that he is a member of the Body of Christ which embraces the whole world. But I contend here that the genesis of these prayer-formulas must be from below, from the ordinary Christians through response to the Word of God. That means that prayer-forms should first appear as charismatic improvisations, subsequently collected and officially sanctioned by ecclesial authority. This is in keeping with the Christian rhythm of prayer. God calls, or initiates a dialogue, through the proclamation of the Word or an event of life. Man responds, but this response is a call to action in the world for the glory of God and man.

Accordingly, most of these formulas would be local, regional, national, hardly universal, simply because universal needs are rare. What is more, the emphasis now is on the local, and not the universal, aspects of liturgy. The forms of prayer which are still in force almost everywhere in Africa are translations — or translations of translations — and were not designed to be definitive but directive: not 'pray in these words' but 'pray like this'. Charismatic improvisation derives its validity from the universal priesthood which every Christian derives from Christ and not primarily from official sanction. Here again the emphasis is on the popular rather than the clerical dimension.

Most prayers of Christ recorded in the Bible are occasioned by response to an experience of faith. The Bible stands. It is the greatest source of prayer for the Church. But a given church, while not neglecting hierarchical directives, could select from the Bible those parts which best express and nourish its trust in God. . . . Prayer . . . should be a personal expression of one's feelings in community with other persons to God. It should be a communion of men and God. It should be a celebration. The celebration of the liturgy is a sharing of experiences. Your life experience is mine or becomes mine as we share in the Word and in the Eucharist. Here, then, everyone ought to feel at home as, for instance, the family feels at a meal after a long day of separation by work. Liturgy is not magic and should not be made to appear as such. The idiom and symbols and gestures used there must not portray a magical picture. Instead of waving a hand in the air and calling it a benediction, for example, could we not, quite significantly, replace it with some sort of physical contact, such as placing of hands on the head? What does the kissing of the altar signify in Africa? Has the use of incense been sufficiently explained, understood and accepted? Is the striking of the breast a sign of contrition or defiance? This is just to indicate how necessary a scrutiny of the whole liturgy is to see the relevance of its symbols, gestures and idiom to Africa.

23 A Cultural Model for Christian Prayer
Raymond Arazu

*Raymond Arazu is a Roman Catholic priest and religious
from Nigeria. He is a member of the Congregation of the
Holy Ghost and was born a member of the Igbo tribe.
Continuing the same line of thinking as Laurenti Magesa in
the preceding extract, Fr. Arazu suggests that there are
further lessons to be learned from African traditional prayer.
In this article, first published in 1972, he suggests that the
Ozo initiation rituals of his people, the Igbo, could become a
model for Christian prayer.*

God wants our image of him, our idea of him, to be subject
to the law of death. He pronounced the sentence himself. He
made man in his own image. Man wanted to become God
and not just remain an image. That effort is described by the
Yahwist as the eating of the forbidden fruit. 'You shall die'
became a terrifying reality for God's image, man. Man, the
imago Dei, was driven out of Paradise, out of the primeval,
maternal womb, to face the stark certainty of 'You shall die'.
The tree of life is beyond his reach.

The reality that is God cannot be achieved by human
effort. The builders of the Tower of Babel were the first Pela-
gians. They wanted to get to God by human effort. Those
who want to achieve God, to get attached to him in their sub-
jective psychology in an experimental fashion, are still
building the Tower of Babel. Their language is unintelligi-
ble to other men, for their ideas are fixed, fossilized. God
will never be contained in man's idea.

It is man himself, the whole man, body-spirit, that is the
authentic image of God. A human being, man or woman,
slave or free, from any tribe, from any race, in front of me, is
the authentic image of God. The human being takes precedence over every holy picture as *theotokos* (God-bearer). You,
yourself, as a body-spirit-being, are nearer to God and to
what God is than your ideas and images of God. You have a
higher level of being than your ideas have. And God is being

par excellence. To relegate God to the level of abstraction, to pin-point him psychologically, has adverse effects on man's concept of himself.

It seems to me that that is the main cause of what they call crisis in the religious life. The concept the religious have of man is the image of a fossilized idea of God. There must be something wrong with any (religious) congregation that has no attraction for young people. The fault is not with the young as such. The human image as projected by such a congregation is deficient in the light of all that science has discovered about man. There seems to be so many religious people to whom the death of God should be preached so that they may make an effort to return to man and to the living God.

The two commandments of love of God and love of man are explained in a rather disturbing manner by the author of the First Epistle of St. John. 'Anyone who says I love God and hates his brother is a liar, since a man who does not love the brother that he can see cannot love God whom he has never seen.' It is very difficult to fulfil this commandment in a religious community because everyone there knows this quotation and knows when the neighbour is trying to make use of another neighbour in order to be accounted charitable before the imagined God. The young religious can — and ought to — transcend the fossilized ideas of God in many ways. It is still part of love to wake sleepers when the sun is up, even if they do not like it. To get a kick through the blanket is still love! We must trust young people. They can get around to work when they are well informed.

The height of contemplation coincides with 'the Word was made Flesh'. It was the privileged moment in world history when reason was completely transcended and God became one of us. The pagan is confused. We blink violently and proceed to wrap the naked child in the manger with swaddling clothes of new images and ideas of God. Mary handled the reality, which is always too concrete for sophisticated tastes. But all that happened 2,000 years ago!

We must not forget that the Yahwist account of creation described God as a potter moulding man (Adam) from clay (*adamah*), and breathing into his nostrils the breath of God. That was how man became a living being, a material spirit or spiritual matter. That was how God became represented in visible creation according to the abstract terminology of the Priestly account of the origin of man. That, too, was how the mystery of the Incarnation began. Man is not a pagan spirit that broke loose from the great beyond and is chained in individual bodies as a punishment. No. Man has a divine origin. Man is body-spirit and has a divine origin as such. Man is the authentic image of God. Man is 'the God we can see'. To explain man's resemblance to God as physical or moral is to go back to abstraction. Man's resemblance to God involves man as a body-spirit-being. The resemblance cannot be explained philosophically. It is a religious resemblance.

The animist rites of initiation — especially the Ozo title-taking phenomenon in Igbo culture — captured this truth long before the Christian message came to modern Africa. The Ozo chief achieves union with spirit (God) and becomes spiritualized, deified, through prolonged, mysterious and trying rites of initiation. This has nothing to do with puberty initiation. The candidate must be an adult. In one locality he is buried alive for some hours. A plank is placed over the shallow grave and earth is thrown on it. The death wail is started and the burial ceremonies are performed. When the uninitiated retire, he is exhumed and whitewashed with chalk. In another locality the Ozo chief-to-be goes into seclusion for weeks (twenty-four days) and has to take a ritual bath in the sacred river at the dead of night before he comes back to the land of the living. Through the Ozo initiation the candidate does not become the priest of any god. He becomes man, and no longer man. The word for man in Igbo is *mma-du*, meaning literally 'let goodness exist'.

An old Igbo contemplative animist confided to me once that Chukwu (God) looked on the world he had made and pronounced the sentence: 'Let goodness exist' — *Mma-du*! Th result of this order from Chukwu was man as we see him today. Man's essence is an order from the Supreme Being: 'Let goodness exist'. The name is the nature. But man committed original sin in the fact that he pronounces his name without a pause in the middle of the word. Man sinned when he pronounced his name without thought. That sin is the result of all the other evils that surround man. Man is in too much of a hurry to pronounce his own name correctly. Moral suicide! When man does not understand what he is, how can he understand anything else? In the solitude imposed by the Ozo ritual initiation the candidate learns to pronounce 'man' with deliberation. He sees that his very nature is a statement from the Supreme Being: 'Let goodness exist'. The man who does not meditate, who does not contemplate, will never realize what man means. Such a person lives in such a way that he should not be called *mma-du* but *njo-du* — 'let badness exist'. Through the rites of initiation, the Ozo chief attains the meaning of man. Man in his concrete existence is the nearest resemblance to divinity. The resemblance is neither moral nor physical. These concepts are not adequate in this matter. Man's resemblance to God is religious. The Ozo rites of initiation take in every aspect of human activity, politicial, social, religious, etc. The Ozo chief, after the initiation, becomes the leader of the democratic village. But he is not a pagan priest. He is *imago Dei (deorum?)*.

Christianity took its origin from such a phenomenon, where one who was supposed to be a mere human being smashed all human ideas and images of God through his death, resurrection and ascension, in the course of which his identity came to noon-day light as both 'Lord and Christ'. The pagan is confused once more while the believer keeps blinking. The reality is beyond ideas and images. It is there without swaddling clothes — naked!

The young religious must be led into the depth of the mystery of salvation. The novitiate must become a kind of Ozo initiation where the novice learns to pronounce 'man' correctly. It is mainly in the sacraments that we go beyond the ideas and images of God and of Christ. In the sacraments, the reality that took place 2,000 years ago takes hold of man here and now. In the sacraments the ideas and the images of God that result from contemplation are transcended in a symbolic burying-alive of the recipient, who thus attains Christ and becomes man in the original sense of Genesis (1:26 — 27):

God said, 'Let us make man in our own image, in the

likeness of ourselves, and let them be masters of the fish of the sea, the birds of heaven, the cattle, all the wild beasts. . . .' God created man in the image of himself; in the image of God he created him; male and female he created them.

Contemplation ends up in sacrament. Without it man would perform the sacraments without deliberation, the original sin in the Ozo system. In the sacraments man meets Christ and opens his eyes to the reality outside his head, outside his thinking heart: it is the concrete existing man, and not the image or the idea in the head, that represents God.

24 Spirituality and World Community
Kenneth Kaunda

*The ethnic cultures — or ways of life — of traditional Africa
have one important common feature, a strong experience
and sense of community. The commitment to an African
way of life, therefore, is necessarily a commitment to
community life. President Kenneth Kaunda of Zambia
makes the community sense of the African the basis for a
political philosophy in which men and women of all
cultures recognize each other as brothers and sisters. This is
the Zambian philosophy of Humanism. However, the
President makes it clear that the success of this philosophy
depends on a religious attitude, and on the concept of the
soul as the centre of a network of relationships.*

The humanist believes that men belong to each other; that
no man is an island, self-entire. His estimate of Man is based
on the assumption that no race or class or group has a
monopoly of all human gifts and powers. Each natural
group has certain weaknesses which need the reinforcement
of the strength of others, and it is through human interaction that Man achieves his potential. Segregation denies the
richness and variety of the human heritage. It proposes the
monotony of a garden filled with flowers of a single colour,
the loneliness of a community of only one sex, or the impo-
tence of a body comprising only a single organ.

For the humanist the fundamental human right is the
right to love and to be loved. Segregation, on the other hand,
generates hate because it strengthens fear of the unknown,
and it is a truth of human nature that we tend to hate rather
than love that which we fear through ignorance.

Of course, there is such a thing as natural human community, but the basis on which individuals come together in
groups has nothing to do with such artificial similarities as
skin-colour, but rather with the drive of people with a common history to achieve a common destiny. Increasingly, in
the modern world, even the nation-state is being found defec-

tive as a vehicle of human destiny and the first slender fila-
ments of world community are being woven between men
everywhere. Humanism, therefore, harnesses the power of
historical destiny, whilst *apartheid* is fighting against history, and it is a matter of record that those nations which
have attempted to resist history have been swept aside. . . .

I am hesitant to use the term, but I do believe in the need
to propagate a religion of humanity which in no way
negates the morally elevating aspects of the great world religions but correlates their deepest insights into Man's
nature. I envisage the service of God as being most practi-
cally effected through the service of one's fellow men. No
earthly idol, whether the state, the family or anything else,
ought to take priority over respect for mankind; they are
only worthy of respect in so far as they are images of the
human spirit, enshrine its presence and aid its self-fulfilment, but where the cult of these idols seeks to usurp the
place of the spirit, they should be put aside. They become
dead husks, destined to decay. No injunctions of old creeds,
religious, political, social or cultural, are valid if they dimin-
ish Man. Science even, one of the chief idols of the modern
world, must not be allowed to serve any lesser goal than the
greater humanizing of Man. War, the needless taking of
human life, cruelty of all kinds, whether committed by the
state, or the individual, the degradation of any human
being, class or race, under whatever specious plea of justification, are intolerable crimes against the religion of mankind, abominable to its ethical mind, forbidden by its
primary tenets, to be fought against always and tolerated
not at all. Man must be sacred to man. The body of Man is to
be respected, made immune from violence and outrage, protected by science against disease and preventable death. The
life of Man is to be held sacred, preserved, ennobled and
uplifted. The heart of Man is to be held sacred also, given
scope for love, protected against dehumanizing influences
that would turn it into some biological machine. The mind
of man is to be released from all bonds, given freedom and
opportunity to use the full range of its powers in the service
of mankind.

All this I believe with an intensity that moves me to terrible anger when I see Man misused, degraded and abandoned

to the mercy of impersonal forces. These apparently abstract sentiments have, in fact, been the driving power behind much that mankind has accomplished through men and women of many races and all ages. In so far as society has been humanized, its concepts of works, law and punishment, its treatment of the weak and underprivileged have been enlightened; it is the exponents of the religion of mankind who have accomplished these things. They have stimulated philanthropy and charity, put a curb on oppression and minimized its most brutal aspects.

It is from this source deep in the soul of the individual that I believe the creative power to achieve world community must come. And the great enemy of the religion of mankind is egotism, whether of the individual, the race or the nation. Until enough men recognize that the fulfilment of the human spirit is impossible in isolation from the fulfilment of all men, then the most pessimistic predictions about the future of the human race will prove accurate, and for all the dazzling light of science we shall enter a new Dark Age.

So what I am trying desperately hard to impress on you . . . is that no mechanical, political or administrative unity of mankind is remotely possible until the sacred value of Man possesses not only your imaginations as a vision, but also your wills as a programme of action and a way of life.

The old evangelists like my revered father, who never lived to witness the marvels of this modern age, were, for all their blessed simplicity, utterly justified in their claim that all social, political and economic programmes for the betterment of the human condition finally depend on a fundamental change in human nature. As a boy, I remember him thundering from that pulpit in Lubwa, that all men must be brothers, but how is that possible unless they acknowledge a common Father? True brotherhood, which is the final, far-off goal of the human race, is ultimately dependent upon what my Indian friends would call soul force. Brotherhood exists only in the soul and by the soul. I can exist by nothing else. For all men are not brothers by biological kinship, human association or intellectual agreement. They are brothers at the level of the soul; and all forms of human unity, political, social and economic, can only be expressions of soul brotherhood; never substitutes for it.

My theologian friends tell me it is unfashionable these days to talk about the soul. So much the worse for theology! For I believe that the soul is the seat of all social virtue. When the soul claims freedom, it is the freedom of its self-development, the self-development of the divine. Man in all his being. When it claims equality, what is being claimed is that same freedom equally for all and the recognition of the same soul, the same divinity in all human beings. When it strives for brotherhood, it is founding that equal freedom of self-development on a common aim, a common life, a unity of mind and feeling.

So when I talk of the human soul, I am using that term to describe the primal essence of a man as the centre of a network of relationships with others. This is why I contrast ego with soul and regard egotism as the great enemy of mankind. When the ego claims liberty, it arrives only at competitive individualism. When it asserts equality, it succeeds only in creating a mechanical uniformity of society which suppresses the infinite variations of human types from whose interaction creativity, beauty and excitement flourish. Hence a society of egotists which pursues liberty is unable to achieve equality; the same society which aims at equality is obliged to sacrifice liberty. For the egotistic personality to speak of fraternity is to talk of things contrary to its nature. The egotism of men can be neutralized, balanced and harmonized in such a way that some kind of community is possible. Obviously this is so, otherwise I would not be writing this and you would not be reading it! But I am sure that the apparently inviolate law of growth and decay which characterizes societies at present can only be broken and some form of lasting and all-embracing community created when sufficient people realize that the revolution which really has lasting effect is not that which is achieved from the outside in — that is by violent economic and political change, altering human nature — but from the inside out — human nature being transformed so that men create societies worthy of their stature as Man made in the image of God.

And I end this rather odd discussion about the possibility of world community by putting to you my conviction that the challenge which will face (the younger) generation when it rules the world can be stated in a question simple to express, though desperately difficult to answer. How can we get men to live from their soul, instead of their ego? I would suggest, with the diffidence of one who will have had his day and ceased to be, that in this struggle the role of religion will be crucial. It would not be putting it too highly to claim that if, as is commonly assumed, religion is finished, then Man is finished, and the alternatives before you will be stark — atomic extinction or the unification of the world on the basis of some form of dictatorship in which a rich and powerful minority hold down a poor and powerless majority.

I do not believe this is what God intends the shape of the future to be, nor it is the kind of world I want you to inherit. So I must do what I can and put my faith in you to do the rest.

25 Trinity and Community
Christopher Mwoleka

Ujamaa ('familyhood') is the name of Tanzania's political philosophy and, as its name implies, it takes the family community as the model for community co-operation at village level, and ultimately at all other levels. Bishop Christopher Mwoleka is known to many people inside and outside Tanzania as the 'ujamaa Bishop'. This is because he has taken his country's philosophy seriously and spends several days each week, living and working in an ujamaa village. In this article he shares with us his own Christian interpretation of ujamaa. For him it is participating in the life of the Divine Community — the Holy Trinity. Christopher Mwoleka is Roman Catholic Bishop of Rulenge in north-western Tanzania.

I am dedicated to the ideal of *ujamaa* because it invites all men, in a down-to-earth, practical way, to imitate the life of the Trinity, which is a life of sharing. The three divine persons share everything in such a way that they are not three gods but only one. And Christ's wish is: 'That they (his followers) may be one as we are one. With me in them and you in me. May they be completely one. . . .'

Have you ever considered why Christianity is differeent from all other religions? All great religions believe in one God. It is only Christianity which believes that this one God is three persons. Why should God have revealed this mystery to us? Christ referred to it many times. It is a pity that many people find it very difficult to understand what this mystery is all about. Many Christian do not know what to do with it, except that it must be believed. It is a dogma they cannot apply to their daily life. So they push it aside to look for interesting devotions elsewhere.

The school children in a catechism class find the Trinity interesting because it is to them a riddle to play with. Teachers look for examples to illustrate the mystery — without success. Theologians have made the Trinity a kind of intellectual exercise, speculating on it until their heads get dizzy. We are told that Saint Augustine almost lost his head trying to grasp what the Trinity was all about until the angel came to his rescue at the sea-shore — which really means that he gave up!

I think we have problems in understanding the Holy Trinity because we approach the mystery from the wrong side. The intellectual side is not the best side to start with. We try to get hold of the wrong end of the stick, and it never works. The right approach to the mystery is to imitate the Trinity. We keep repeating the mistake that Philip made by asking: 'Rabbi, show us the Father!' Christ was dismayed by this request and rebuked Philip: 'Philip, have I been with you so long and you have not known me? He who has seen me has seen the Father. How can you say: Show us the Father? Do you not believe that I am in the Father and the Father in me?' Then Christ continued to say: 'He who believes in me will also do the works that I do, and greater works than these will he do.'

On believing in this mystery, the first thing we should have done was to imitate God, then we would ask no more questions, for we would understand. God does not reveal himself to us for the sake of speculation. He is not giving us a riddle to solve. He is offering us life. He is telling us: 'This is what it means to live; now begin to live as I do.' What is the one and only reason why God revealed this mystery to us if it is not to stress that life is not life at all unless it is shared? If we would once begin to share life in all its aspects, we would soon understand what the Trinity is all about and rejoice.

If, in the Catholic Church, there is something faulty with our methods of presenting the message of the Gospel or Good News it is this: we have not presented religion as a sharing of life. All that people know about religion is the carrying out of commandments — ten commandments of God and seven commandments of the Church, reducing Christianity almost to the same category as the natural religions. We have behaved as though God had not revealed his inner, intimate life to us. What we should do is to put the Trinity before men, not in abstract ideas but in concrete facts of our human earthly life: present the life of the Trinity as shared and lived by us Christians here and now.

Why did God, upon creating men, not put them straight into heaven, but instead put them here on earth? The reason why we should first have to wait here for a number of years before going to heaven would seem to be that we should practise and acquire some competence in the art of sharing life. Without this practice we are apt to mess up things in heaven! So we are here for practice. And for this practice, God has given us toys with which to practise, as children do. Before children grow up and build real houses, own real farms, rear cows or drive cars, they first pass through a period of practising with toys those things which they see their parents doing. For toys God has given us material things. Material things, therefore, are not accidental. They are necessary for our condition here on earth. We cannot do without them. Material things must not be despised or ignored, but must be used as training equipment for the job that we have to do — eternally. All I want to say is this: it is by sharing the earthly goods that we come to have an idea of what it is like to share the life of God. As long as we do not know how to share earthly goods, as God would have us do, it is an illusion to imagine that we know what it is to share the life of the Trinity which is our destiny. If you cannot manage with toys, nobody is going to entrust you with the real thing.

The question is: Have we imitated the Holy Trinity in sharing earthly goods? Have Christians tried to do this in all earnest? Could I truthfully say: 'All mine are thine and thine are mine' to each and all? This is what we are supposed to imitate (John 17:10). Then in what sense can we be said to be practising to live the life of God? How can we dare to profess the religion of the Trinity? The Fathers of the Second Vatican Council rightly made a confession: 'We Christians have concealed the true face of God and of religion more than we have revealed it' (*Gaudium et Spes* 19).

You know how those who deny God and religion define life. Let us quote the extremists — the Marxists. They try to figure out what life should be at its best and dream a society in which 'each will give according to his capacity and receive according to his needs'. We know that they have made fantastic efforts and that they have not succeded. They have used methods that we do not, and cannot, approve. But their vision and their dream could be said to aim at a transformation from *cupiditas* to *caritas* — from self-centred

love to other-centred love. It could be a Trinitarian life
expressed in human and material terms. If the Marxists fail
to achieve their goal, the main reason would seem to be that
they try to impose their ideal upon men from the outside,
without the necessary, corresponding, interior dispositions.
If we Christians claim to possess these interior dispositions
of charity by the grace of Christ, then we should be able to
express them in a concrete material way in a manner that
would make the Marxists wonder at our success. Would this
not constitute a meeting-point between us and them, or at
least a point of dialogue?

Tanzanians are not Marxists, nor do they deny God.
ujamaa is aimed at sharing life in as many of its aspects as
possible. The government is trying to set up social structures that are viable for this kind of life. I think it is the duty
of Church members to supply the interior dispositions
needed for this kind of life as the Second Vatican Council
has exhorted us: 'The Church admonishes her own sons to
give internal strength to human associations which are just'
(*Gaudium et Spes* 42). So in Tanzania Providence has
already provided a new horizon for the apostolate that
would bring all men under the rule of Christ. This is why I
shall not let this chance slip out of my hands!

26 An Ujamaa Theology
Camillus Lyimo

*Camillus Lyimo was a Roman Catholic theological student
when he wrote this article about creating a theology centred
on the major tenets of Tanzania's political philosophy. The
author comes from central Tanzania and was then studying
at a major seminary near Tabora. He sketches for us a
theology based on human equality, community-living,
freedom and mutual love.*

By the term 'an *ujamaa* theology' I wish to talk about the
possibility of creating a theology centred upon the basic
belief in the equality of men, sense of community, freedom,
sharing and real love. These five elements are consonant
with any real Christian living. Thus they are uniquely relevant for the *ujamaa* Christians. They are part and parcel of a
sound theology because they are found both in the Scrip-
tures and in the official teachings of the Church.

For that matter, it is not meant to be a theology of *ujamaa*
politics or *ujamaa* economics. Yet, certain overtones of
ujamaa politics will prevail, because we are never completely free from the ties of our political and economic envir-
onment. An *ujamaa* theology, therefore, is an attempt to
consider how man, in his capacity to share as a being-in-
community, ordered by divine will, can truly make life
worth living on this earth of grass and dust, thus answering
God's call in Creation: 'Fill the earth and conquer it' (Gen.
1:28).

Theology is born of ideas and reflections. Unless the intellectuals of Africa in all fields share ideas and enrich each
other there will scarcely be creativity. Shared reflections give
way to a system of patterned thought. This in turn gives way
to conviction and conviction to action. *Ujamaa* theology
calls the politician, the theologian, the philosopher, the
poet, the musician, the rural farmer, the tribal elder and the
woman, indeed everybody, to the sharing of ideas. Perhaps
it is due to the inadequate sharing of ideas among ourselves

(Africans) that render us silent and dependent on the thought of others, such that there is no mutual, spontaneous enrichment. Father Aylward Shorter is right when he says that the theses of Africans lie scattered in the university libraries of Europe and America, and their authors have not been able to influence each other.

Every theology has its marked characteristics which depend upon the place of origin, the Church's activity in that place, the historical circumstances and so forth. What then are the possible and conspicuous characteristics of an *ujamaa* theology?

An *ujamaa* theology has to be historical because it is obliged to take into account the historical circumstances proper to her. The history we now make by raising the standards of living of our people points to the future. It is the history characteristic of an *ujamaa* theology. Theology has to be born within it. Why not? The term *ujamaa* began to be used in Tanzania. It bears fruit within the history of Tanzania. And history plunges us into the past, situates us in the present and directs our hopes into the future. The future must be better than the present or otherwise there is no reason to look up to it. And since our *ujamaa* theology concerns man's sharing power in community in terms of tangible development and liberation, doubtlessly, this growth takes place in our history. History is a process towards a definite reality. We must have faith in our history or else the reality to which we aspire becomes illusory. For me, history is a vital characteristic of this proposed theology, because all theology has in fact become history, and our point of reference will always be history.

Sharing is part of the whole economy of salvation. That is why man is saved in a community. It is also an affirmation of the basic equality of men. To be a member of a community means to enter into the sharing of relationships; into the sharing of wealth or riches, of talents and especially, work. It means also sharing the burdens, the failures as well as the successes of that community. Thus a theology built on the reality of community must be characteristically about sharing. *Ujamaa* by itself is distributive. That is, sharing in the concrete. It means mutual, brotherly enrichment.

The concrete man is 'man-in-community'. This is

affirmed by the Church's teaching:

> God did not create man for life
> in isolation, but for the formation
> of social unity. . . .
> This communitarian character is
> developed and consummated in the
> work of Jesus Christ. For the
> very Word made flesh willed to share
> in the human fellowship.

Further illumination on the community nature of man is based on the life of the Trinity. Though for us knowledge of the life of the Trinity is indeed little, yet we can say that the most perfect community or *ujamaa* is the Trinity. The Trinity establishes God as community. Jesus Christ revealed the Trinity to us. God wished to share with humanity and the entire creation his own community life in the person of Jesus Christ who became consubstantial with us. Our life is a shared life in the Trinity. But for us, we now ask: How is this possible outside — what is for us — a tangible, shared, existential, community life on this earth? It seems quite acceptable that a movement which is committed to the realization of community life is concordant with the 'plan of God'. That is why, in Tanzania today, the Church is rethinking herself. She now moves to establish small, Christian communities, and to my mind, a sound theology behind this process can only be envisaged in the new way of life proposed by *ujamaa*.

An *ujamaa* theology must be love-centred. Without love, community is meaningless and sharing is impossible. By love we mean Christian love or brotherly love. Love is the place in which we live, move and exist (Acts 17:28). It is a dynamic, transforming power within man. It is the basis for understanding the nature of human community. In a community there is not true love outside God. Our personal encounter with our fellow men is our encounter with God. This comes true in love. Loving one's neighbour is loving God. Jesus Christ taught us to love in the concrete, that is to concretize our charity, to liberate man from his afflictions. According to this way of thinking, *ujamaa* efforts become salvific. In love, the freedom of each individual will be respected, safeguarded and promoted. The theology of the Church, indeed the Church herself will become the confirmation of the love of God to all men.

My last proposed characteristic of an *ujamaa* theology is practical prophetism. To be sound, any theology must be prophetic and practical. The Church by nature is prophetic. Hence her theology is prophetic. The prophets of the Old Testament were practical and realistic. In the New Testament Jesus Christ was the prophet *par excellence*. He was critical. He did not simply accept everything that the people of his time considered to be ideal. Paul, speaking to the Corinthians about prophets, has this to say:

> The man who prophesies talks to other people, for their improvement, their encouragement and their consolation . . . , he does so for the benefit of the community. (1 Cor. 14:3-4).

In the process of creating human communities aberrations do occur. Prophets are needed to criticize in order to approve things and that is where *ujamaa* theology seeks to be prophetic and practical. To reiterate, this characteristic springs from the nature of the Church. Thus the task of an *ujamaa* Christian, in the building of human communities, is to criticize, not as an onlooker, but rather as one consciously and deliberately working hard here and now to share with others and bring about the transformation truly desired by God.

27 Living and Dead in Fellowship with God
Harry Sawyerr

Harry Sawyerr, from Sierra Leone and one of Black Africa's leading Protestant theologians, makes a vital point about the African understanding of community. It is this: the community in African tradition includes the departed as well as the living. Harry Sawyerr discusses this idea from the Christian standpoint and concludes that the doctrine of the Communion of Saints can accommodate such a belief. Moreover, there are excellent precedents for this in the Bible. Living and dead are made one through their fellowship with God and the life of the Spirit which is the community-principle of the Church.

The African community embraces the living, the unborn and the dead. Christians know of the Church militant on earth, the Church triumphant in heaven, and the Church expectant in a state between the first two. In the Canon of the Mass they pray at the *Memento Domine* that God may 'grant some part and fellowship with the holy apostles and martyrs . . . into whose company we beseech thee to admit us. . . .' Because Christians have entered into a mystical relation with Christ, they are exhorted to live 'as those risen from the dead' (Rom. 6:13). This exhortation is a corollary of the fact that at baptism they are raised (from the dead by the Holy Spirit) to walk in newness of life. Second, in this resurrection life, they could attain the state of oneness (*henosis*) with Christ in which they could say like St. Paul:

I have been crucified with Christ: the life I
now live is not my life, but the life which Christ
lives in me; and my present bodily life is lived by
faith in the Son of God, who loved me and sacrificed
himself for me . . . . (Gal. 2:20ff.)

Here the Christian is in symbiosis with Jesus Christ our elder brother, the first-born of many brethren. Unlike the ancestral dead of the Africans, Jesus Christ, once dead, now lives. Every true Christian has a personal experience of him as a life-giving spirit, returned to his place of glory in the Godhead. He also knows from the testimony of the Bible that Jesus Christ was seen after his resurrection by up to five hundred brethren (1 Cor. 15:6; Acts 10:40ff.).

Africans, on the other hand, whilst claiming that their ancestors are alive in the spirit do so without any concrete evidence. This belief in their existence is based primarily on dreams and not on any empirical or theological grounds. (We may here observe that dreams, so far as we can tell, are purely subconscious commentaries on the dreamers.) But these dreams determine the life of the people who behave according to the dictates of those as-it-were risen from the dead. Their day-to-day life is accordingly so ordered as to please the ancestors. Disasters and illnesses are attributed to their anger, and success in one's undertakings is the outcome of their approval and therefore of their blessing. The ancestors thus come to be regarded as the co-guardians with the cultic spirits of the mores of the community. Dr. Baeta succinctly states this relationship when he said at a United Christian Council Conference in Accra in 1955, ' . . . whatever others may do in their own countries, our people live with their dead'.

All of us Africans feel that our deceased parents and other ancestors are close to us. In the present context, therefore, Christian doctrinal teaching should be directed towards first presenting the Church as a corporate body with a unique solidarity transcending by far anything akin to it in pagan African society; and second discovering a means of preserving the tribe, the solidarity of living and dead, as Africans understand that relationship, but in a new idiom, that of the community of the Church. In any case, ancestors are thought of in relation to their tribes or clans or families. They could therefore be readily embraced within the framework of the universal Church and be included in the communion of saints.

This suggestion poses *in se* an important theological problem in view of the fact that Christian prayers are said on behalf of 'the faithful departed'. Non-Christians are thus excluded. We would however ask: Is there no room for including non-Christians in our prayers? We do so for the living; as for example when we pray for the peace of the world. Is it wrong then to do the same for the dead? Our interpretation of the feeling of Christians of New Testament times leads us to the conclusion that they had a real concern for their relatives and compatriots who had died either before the establishment of the Christian Church (in the case of non-Christians) or before the Parousia (in the case of Christians). In particular, we would mention the Matthean record that at the death of Jesus Christ, 'many of God's people arose from sleep and coming out of their graves after his resurrection they entered the Holy City, where many saw them' (Matt. 27:52). Other such references are to the 'baptism for the dead' (1 Cor. 15:29), the *descensus ad inferos* (descent into Hades, 1 Pet. 3:19) and to the dead in Christ rising at the Parousia (1 Thess. 4:14-18).

But perhaps more significant than this concern is the inclusion by the writer of the epistle to the Hebrews in 'his roll of heroes' of figures of the past, some of whom he himself must have recognized as very imperfect specimens of humanity . . . like Gideon, Samson and Barak whom C.H. Dodd describes as being 'no better than savages'. We could add Rahab the prostitute to Dodd's list. Dodd goes on to say: 'Their presence in any Christian heaven is incongruous enough', but he also recognizes that 'upon the faith and courage of just such primitive ancestors later achievements rest. They were not perfect, it is true; without us they could not be made perfect. But in the deathless society of the People of God they draw upon the treasury of life to which more enlightened generations have since contributed their experience of the love of God.'

We suggest that Dodd's language is eminently applicable to the African situation in view of the covenant relationship which we described earlier. If the African lives with his dead, he would naturally feel himself in the wrong place if there was no opportunity for him to realize the hoped-for comradeship with his ancestors, just because he had become a Christian. We would, therefore, go on to suggest that the prayers of African Christians might, in the providence of God, lead to the salvation of their pagan ancestors. Indeed, we may justifiably add that it is highly probable that some of the dead for whom the early Christians were baptized had never heard of the promise of salvation through Jesus Christ. At best they had not reponded to the preaching of the Christian Gospel even if they had heard it. How often do we not feel that if some of the current drugs — penicillin, aureomycetin and Salk vaccine for example — had been discovered say, fifty years ago, some of our relatives might not have died when they did. We are inclined to the view that, just as the progress of medicine has been influenced by the fatality caused by certain diseases to our predecessors, so, in the context of the saving work of Jesus Christ, God in his wisdom may have 'made a better plan, that only in company with us should they reach their perfection' (Heb. 11:40). For in Christ there is renovation and fulfilment, not only of sanctified persons, but also of the whole creation; and this transformation takes place within a new world-order whose outward form is vitally significant since it manifests the new organism of Christ. . . .

Christian teaching based on the Incarnation might then, first of all, state that God intends man to be in fellowship with Him (Eph. 2:16-18), and that, through this fellowship with God, we are led into a new fellowship with our fellow men (Eph. 3:6); in other words, that the Incarnation provides the basis for a common life. We can then venerate the ancestors, but not pour libations to them. We may then rightly pray for their souls, and, if we are prepared to accept that their personalities do not perish with death, expect them to feel a concern for us and make intercession to God for us. This interpretation of the state of the ancestral dead would readily dispose of the belief in the reincarnation, because Christian teaching allows for a resurrection life, imparted by God, which admits of the preservation of man's individuality, and rejects any suggestion either of his absorption into the Alone, as the Gnostics and Hindus suggest, or his return to the 'Unformed mass of the race' according to the Akan (Ghana). But this resurrection life is based on the resurrection life of Jesus Christ whom God raised from the dead. His resurrection is the guarantee of ours (1 Cor. 15:12-29). But it begins here and now under the influence of the Holy Spirit. So St. Paul can say to the Roman Christians 'the body is dead because of sin; but the Spirit is life because of righteousness' (Rom. 8:10ff.).

The human spirit infused with the life-giving Spirit of God through baptism assumes the quality we call eternal life. Such a spirit, when the body passes through the experience of physical death, must preserve its capacity to endure. St. Paul also adds the further note that when God's Holy Spirit possesses any man, he will quicken his mortal body. Some may object, and perhaps rightly so, that this discussion is primarily relevant to the man who in this life accepts Jesus Christ as Lord and Saviour. But, once again, we must not predetermine God's attitude to non-Christians. We may rightly and in all humility postulate that, on the final day of judgement, God 'shall be all in all', and pray that all men may have come to grasp his unspeakable love.

28 Humanism and Community in Africa
Kenneth Kaunda

Kenneth Kaunda of Zambia continues here his examination of African traditional community life in order to draw from it the principles for community living in modern African countries. The African traditional community was, he says, a mutual society, an accepting society and an inclusive society. He sees these features not simply as functions of a disappearing social system, but as a fundamental part of the African's psychology.

I believe that the Universe is basically good and that throughout it great forces are at work striving to bring about a greater unity of all living things. It is through co-operation with these forces that Man will achieve all of which he is capable. Those people who are dependent upon, and live in closest relationship with Nature are most conscious of the operation of these forces: the pulse of their lives beats in harmony with the pulse of the Universe. They may be simple and unlettered people and their physical horizons may be strictly limited, yet I believe that they inhabit a larger world than the sophisticated Westerner who has magnified his physical senses through invented gadgets at the price, all too often, of cutting out the dimension of the spiritual.

Only the other evening I was reading in the Book of Psalms. I came across a verse in which the Psalmist is praising God for having 'set his feet in a large room'. Now David came from a pastoral people dependent upon Nature, and though I find some of his ideas about God crude and mistaken, there is a sort of bold sweep to his thinking which comes from inhabiting the 'large room' of Nature, rather than the machine-packed workshop of industrial society. The Psalmist can make a declaration linking God with the Universe in one verse of fifty words. Scientifically orientated modern Man often requires a hundred thousand words to state a thesis concerning some tiny, specialized aspects of truth. Now I know, of course, that these two approaches are not contradictory and I am not denying the importance of the scientific method. But my point is that people in close relationship with Nature are forced to ask big questions however crude their answers might be. I could entertain you for hours retelling the traditional stories of my people I first heard in my childhood, many of which offer ingenious, if somewhat fanciful, explanations of the great riddles of life to which the world's great thinkers have sought solutions.

It is easy, of course, to romanticize Nature, but this is an error more likely to be made by those comfortably protected from it than by people like myself who have experienced its cruellest moods in disease, blight, famine and drought. To be exposed to Nature and to have to live your life at its rhythm develops humility as a human characteristic rather than arrogance. Men are companionable and take the trouble to live harmoniously together because they know that only by acting together can they reap the benefits and try to overcome the hardships of Nature.

Was it not the Luddites in England who went around smashing the new machines of the Industrial Revolution because they could not face the future? I am no Luddite! I welcome all the advantages which Western science and technology have brought to Africa. I even welcome the fact that technology reduces our dependence upon the uncertainties of Nature, in spite of all that I have said. Yet my question is this: Is there any way that my people can have the blessings of technology without being eaten away by materialism and losing the spiritual dimension of their lives? I suppose the answer is that, however intensely we industrialize, the vast majority of the peoples of Africa will still live in close contact with Nature and so keep alive this element in our culture.

The second element in African humanism stems from the structure of the traditional society and its effects upon African psychology. The devoted work of anthropologists has now borne fruit and only the bigot would dismiss tribal society as primitive and chaotic. It is widely recognized that these societies were, in fact, highly organized and delicately balanced in the network of relationships which held their members together. I need not go into great detail since the characteristics of the tribal community are well known. Let me draw attention only to three key factors which reinforce the humanistic outlook.

The tribal society was a mutual society. It was organized to satisfy the basic human needs of all its members and, therefore, individualism was discouraged. Most resources such as land and cattle might be communally owned and administered by chiefs and village headmen for the benefit of everyone. If, for example, a villager required a new hut, all the men would turn to and cut trees to erect the frame and bring grass for thatching. The women might be responsible for making the mud-plaster for the walls and two or three of them would undoubtedly brew some beer so that all the workers would be refreshed after a hot, but satisfying, day's work. In the same spirit, the able-bodied would accept responsibility for tending and harvesting the gardens of the sick and infirm.

Human need was the supreme criterion of behaviour. The hungry stranger could, without penalty, enter the garden of a village and take, say, a bunch of bananas or a mealie cob to satisfy his hunger. His action only became theft if he took more than was necessary to satisfy his needs. For then he was depriving others.

Obviously, social harmony was a vital necessity in such a community where almost every activity was a matter of team work. Hence chiefs and tribal elders had an important judicial and reconciliatory function. They adjudicated between conflicting parties, admonished the quarrelsome and anti-social, and took whatever action was necessary to strengthen the fabric of social life. I should emphasize that this way of life was not a kind of idealized social experiment as may be found in Europe where groups of peoples take themselves off into pleasant rural surroundings in order to avoid the tensions of industrial society. Life in the bush is hard and dangerous and a high degree of social cohesion is necessary for survival. The basic unit of life is not the individual or immediate family (as in industrial societies) but the community. This means that there must be fundamental agreement upon goals and all must act together.

In the second place, the tribal community was an accepting community. It did not take account of failure in an abso-

lute sense. The slow, the inept and incapable were accepted
as a valid element in community life, provided they were
socially amenable. Social qualities weighed much heavier
in the balance than individual achievement. The success-fai-
lure complex seems to me to be a disease of the age of individualism — the result of a society conditioned by the diploma,
the examination and the selection procedure. In the best tribal society people were valued not for what they could
achieve but what they were there. Their contribution, however limited, to the material welfare of the village was acceptable, but it was their presence, not their achievement which
was appreciated.

Take, for instance, the traditional African attitude to old
people. I remember being horrified on the first occasion I
made the acquaintance of that Western phenomenon, the
Old People's Home. The idea that the State, or some voluntary agency, should care for the aged was anathema to me,
for it almost seems to imply that old people are a nuisance
who must be kept out of the way, so that children can live
their lives unhampered by their presence. In traditional
societies old people are venerated and it is regarded as a privilege to look after them. Their counsel is sought on many
matters and, however infirm they might be, they have a valued and constructive role to play in teaching and instruct-
ing their grandchildren. Indeed, to deny a grandparent the
joy of the company of his grandchildren is a heinous sin.
The fact that old people can no longer work, or are not alert
as they used to be, or even have developed the handicap of
senility in no way affects our regard for them. We cannot do
enough to repay them for all they have done for us. They are
embodied wisdom; living symbols of our continuity with
the past.

No doubt a defender of the Western way of life might
retort that institutions for the care of old people are inevitable in large-scale societies and that but for the efforts of the
State and voluntary agencies many old people would starve.
This is undoubtedly true, but it merely serves to underline
my point that in a society which regards person-to-person
relationships as supremely important no one can be so iso-
lated that responsibility for his welface cannot be determin-
edc and assigned.

The experts have all kinds of standards by which they judge the degree of civilization of a people. My own test is this. How does that society treat its old people, and indeed, all its members who are not useful and productive in the narrowest sense? Judged by this standard, the so-called advanced societies have a lot to learn which the so-called backward societies could teach them.

In the third place, the tribal community was an inclusive society. By this I mean that the web of relationships which involved some degree of mutual responsibility was widely spread. I would describe industrial society as an exclusive society because its members' responsibilities are often confined to the immediate family, and I have noted that the family circle may be a self-entire little universe, preventing the acceptance of wider commitments.

Let me give you an example of the inclusiveness of the traditional society. I do not restrict the title 'father' to my male parent. I also address my father's brothers as 'father'. And I call my mother's sisters 'mother' also. Only my father's sisters would I address as 'aunt' and my mother's brothers as 'uncle'. My 'brothers' would include not only the male children of my father but also certain cousins and even members of the same clan who have no blood relationship to me at all. Now this, to the Western mind, very confusing state of affairs, is not merely a matter of terminology. These are not just courtesy titles. With the title 'father', for example, goes all the responsibility of parenthood and, in return, all my 'fathers' receive my filial devotion. Hence no child in a traditional society is likely to be orphaned. Should his literal parents die, then others automatically assume the responsibility for his upbringing. By the same token, no old person is likely to end his days outside a family circle. If his own offspring cannot care for him, then other 'children' will accept the duty and privilege.

The extended family system constitutes a social security scheme which has the advantage of following the natural pattern of personal relationships, rather than being the responsibility of an institution. It also provides for richness in knowledge and experience for those fortunate enough to be part of it. Granted, I have been describing the characteristics of small-scale societies, and it could be argued that such a system would not work where hundreds of thousands of people are gathered together in cities and towns. But the attitudes to human beings which I have set out are not solely a function of social organization. They are now part of the African psychology. I am deeply concerned that this high valuation of Man and respect for human dignity which is a legacy of our tradition should not be lost in the new Africa. However, 'modern' and 'advanced' in a Western sense the new nations of African may become, we are fiercely determined that this humanism will not be obscured. African society has always been Man-centred. We intend that it will remain so.

29 Traditional and Christian Community in Africa
Damian Lwasa

The following article presents another view of African traditional community life, this time from Uganda. Brother Damian Lwasa comes from Buganda, the former kingdom from which the whole of modern Uganda takes its name. Brother Lwasa takes the experience of blood ties among clan members in Buganda as a model for the Mystical Body of Christ, a doctrine developed by Roman Catholic theologians. He then applies the parallel in detail to Christian life. He is obviously presenting an ideal picture of the traditional community and is concentrating on its positive qualities. His purpose is didactic — to show the convergence between African and Roman Catholic ideals.

The community life which is traditional among the African Bantu tribes rests on certain common beliefs concerning the blood-relationships uniting the members of the same clan, and still more the members of a given family group. These beliefs prepare those who hold them to accept the spiritual relationship of Christ. All that it entails in the form of community involvement prepares the African for the Christian community involvement that is incumbent on all Christians as members of the Mystical Body of Christ.

The African belief in a common life, possessed by all the members of the extended family group or clan and received from the common ancestor, is firmly established in most parts of Bantu Africa. There the social structure has always been founded primarily on family and clan (the *kika* system). According to this system, all those persons who descend from, or who can authentically trace their origins to, a common ancestor, not only consider, but also believe, themselves to possess the 'same blood', or in other words, the same common life passed on from one generation to the next. Those who descend from the same ancestor belong to the same clan. As long as the memory of a common ancestor persists, those descending from him belong to the same family group. With each generation, the children and grandchildren widen the family circle, but never break it to start a new family.

Because of their common blood-life lineage and their kin relationship, the members of the extended family (or family group) treat each other as brothers and sisters, and respect, love and help each other. The family circle can be very wide indeed, even extending to whole villages. The importance attached traditionally in African society to blood relationship has aspects which, if judiciously used, may serve as an effective preparation for the Christian belief in our common life in Christ, and consequently for Christian life as brothers in him.

To appreciate our subsequent use of the traditional clan brotherhood and of what it entails to inculcate Christian living in accordance with membership of the Mystical Body of Christ, it is necessary to have a clear idea of what the African means by 'brotherhood in blood'. For the African, 'blood' in this context symbolizes life itself, as it did for the ancient Israelites. The Hebrews considered blood to be the life-principle, the seat of life (as can be seen from Gen. 9:4; Lev. 17:14; Deut. 12:23). So it is with the Africans. When we speak of 'brotherhood in blood' we mean either the interrelatedness of those persons who possess a common life received from the same ancestor, or else the relationship established by a 'blood-bond', called in Luganda (language of the Ganda of Uganda) *omukago*.

For the Christian, blood acquires a salvific significance in the blood of Christ. By freely shedding his blood, Christ laid down his life, gave it up freely for the remission of sins and instituted God's new convenant with his redeemed people — his Church. However, it is to be noted that the fruit of the shedding of Christ's blood was not only the remission of sins, it was also the communication of life — of life in Christ, the divine life of grace. Thus Christ's blood may be said to be the source of the life of his Mystical Body. Since Christ is thus the new Adam, the new head of the human race, he is truly the universal ancestor who gives supernatural life to those who are reborn by the waters of baptism (John 3:3,5; Rom. 5:15). Therefore, all those who receive, and live by his life are 'brothers-in-Christ', because they all possess the same life received from him.

There is another parallel which may be drawn between the common ancestor of the traditional African family group and Christ, the head of the Mystical Body. According to African traditional belief, the spirit of the common ancestor of the clan continues to govern its fortunes. In that line of thought, Christ may be said to be the divine 'ancestor' who continues to govern his Mystical Body and his brethren, the members of his Mystical Body. For Christ 'holds all things in unity (Col. 1:17). 'He is the beginning, he was the first to be born from the dead, so that he should be first in every way; because God wanted all perfection to be found in him and all things to be reconciled through him and for him.' (Col. 1:18-20). He is 'the head that adds strength and holds the whole body together' (Col. 2:19), 'the ruler of everything, the head of the Church' (Eph. 1:23), 'the one who guides all things as he decides by his own will' (Eph. 1:11).

The parallel goes further. The members of the traditional African family group draw inspiration for their conduct from the legendary image of their common ancestor which has come down to them. So also the Christian finds in Christ, his head, his norm of life.

Moreover, the members of the family group believe themselves committed to safeguard their community as such and to ensure its continuance and growth. Indeed, as the Africans see things, it is the common good which primes everything, it takes precedence over the good of the individual. This commitment to safeguard and pass on the life of his family group prepares the African to understand and to accept and fulfil the Christian's obligation to work for the good of the Church as such — an obligation which, as the Church teaches, he accepts at baptism and receives special graces to carry out at his confirmation. By baptism, in fact, he becomes a member of Christ's Mystical Body and incurs the obligation as a member to work for the good of the whole body. At confirmation he receives the guarantee of special help from the Holy Spirit to be active and zealous in his Christian life. The sacraments of baptism and confirmation are the acknowledged sources of the duty of all to devote themselves according to their possibilities to the lay apostolate. Pius XI said in this connection: 'One member must aid the other; none many remain idle; each receives and each must give in his turn.'

Now every Christian receives the supernatural life which circulates in the veins of the Mystical Body, that supernatural life which he himself says he has brought: 'I have come so that they may have life and have it to the full' (John 10:10); and every Christian must consequently pass on this life to others who possess it not at all or only in a slight degree, and perhaps only in outward appearance.

The traditional African family-group has from time immemorial been a well-knit brotherly community. It was characterized by life-together, by personal commitment to the group. The group members threw themselves heart and soul into the life of their group. Manifestly this traditional total commitment of the member of his group is invaluable as a preparation for Christian community living.

The commitment of the individual to his family-group embraced his whole life, but we may distinguish in particular the following domains:

— the religious domain: on certain occasions all the group members gathered together for the worship of the true God and for the cult to be paid to the ancestors, and also to remember the dead;
— the economic domain: agricultural work of certain kinds calling for the co-operation of many, the building and repair of houses, land-clearance, fishing and hunting;
— the social domain: interest in, and material help given on the occasion of betrothals, marriages, births, and initiation and education of children, mourning for the dead, social gatherings;
— the defensive and offensive wars: to defend and promote the interests of the clan;
— group councils of the men: to discuss the affairs of the group;
— meetings of the women: in which they discussed the affairs proper to them.

The participation of the group members in the daily life and activities of the group under the authority of the chief showed that adults knew how to accept discipline and that the young were initiated into it by its enforcement. African traditional community involvement is 'materially' Christian. It makes us think of the community involvement of the early Christians as it is described in the Acts of the Apostles. It needs only grace and Christian motivation to become the Christian community involvement required by membership to the Mystical Body of Christ, though the family circle would have to be widened to include all men.

The African traditional habit of working in all kinds of ways for the good of others is obviously in itself an excellent preparation for the practice of Christian charity. However, there are certain forms of the individual's traditional participation in the life of his group which are particularly valuable in his initiation to Christian involvement in parallel sectors of Christian community life. We note some of them.

In the life of the African, religious worship is not only a personal but also a community act. Traditionally there are occasions when the members of the family group meet together to render homage in some way to the Creator (Katonda in Luganda), apart from the community cult to be paid to the spirits of the group. Religious customs are changing under the influence of Christianity, but in Buganda (homeland of the Ganda of Uganda) such meetings were traditional in time of war to implore the protection of God on the warriors. Also when twins were born, the group-members used to meet together to thank God for this great blessing. In times of epidemic and famine, they gathered together to beg God's help. It was a widespread custom, still existing among the old people, for the head of the group as such, and for the heads of households to invoke the Creator's blessing at sunrise and at sunset on the members of the group or household. Similarly, it was the custom for the head of the family group at the close of a meeting attended by all the men of the group to discuss some important matter, to pray over the group, asking God's blessing on it, and for peace and prosperity for it. In northern and eastern Uganda, meetings involving the worship of the Creator are the practice at the beginning of the sowing and harvesting seasons.

The traditional practice of community worship and the sense of community religious responsibility underlying it manifestly dispose the African to enter fully into the spirit and practice of Christian community worship, especially in the community offering of the Sacrifice of the Mass, and should be used to inculcate into African Christians the true liturgical spirit which is communitarian. The traditional responsibility of the heads of groups and households in religious worship should also be preserved and strengthened in Christian heads of groups and households, for their conversion to Christianity does not bring their responsibility in the religious domain to an end, but gives them the means of fulfilling their obligations in a much more excellent way.

It is traditional African belief that death does not sever completely the relations between a dead member of a family-group and its living members. The dead members continue to be interested in their group and to intervene in its life. Also the living members must continue to respect the dead members who, when alive, had authority, for example parents; and this respect is to be shown by the fulfilment of their wishes. Moreover, death does not mean the perpetual separation of the deceased from the other members of the group. The members are reunited after their death with those who have gone before them. These beliefs are expressed in numerous practices. The help of the deceased members of the group is invoked in time of need — in sickness, danger, drought, famine, when important decisions are to be taken and so on. For this purpose, sacrifices are offered to them. Similarly, sacrifices are offered to placate dead members of the group who are thought to have been offended in some way by the living.

These beliefs and practices may be used to introduce the African Christian to the Church teaching about the communion existing between the members of Christ's Mystical Body still on earth and those in heaven, and the power of the latter to help their brethren of the Church militant. They may also be used to inculcate into the neo-African Christian the habit of invoking the help of the saints. This traditional African belief in the intercommunion and solidarity of the living members of the group with the deceased will also help the African Christian to understand his duty of helping the souls in Purgatory. This will not be entirely new to him. After the death of a member of his family-group and before his burial, it is the custom for the members of the group who live close by to sleep on the floor to expiate for the misdeeds of the dead person.

Underlying the traditional African beliefs we are now considering is faith in the immortality of the soul and in a future life. There is no need to insist on the importance of this in introducing the African to Christian beliefs in this matter.

Traditionally, the members of the family group are extremely devoted to the vitality and growth of their group. Marriage is above all the means of bringing increase to it, so that the fertility of women is a cause for rejoicing, while sterility is considered a curse. Children are a blessing. Deaths are occasions of mourning for all.

The above devotedness of the African to the life and increase of his group naturally prepares him to be actively interested in the vitality and development of the Mystical Body of Christ to which he vitally belongs. He will easily understand that marriage is the means of giving increase to that Body, and children of God. Baptisms will be for him social occasions, the incorporation of new members into the local Christian family. Holy Communion will be the strengthening of the life of Christ in the Christian community and in each of its members, and the strengthening of the bond between them.

Traditionally the upbringing of the children of the family group is the concern not only of the parents, but of all the adult members of the group. As occasion arises, they teach the children the habits and practices of courtesy and good manners of usage in the group, and the respect and obedience to be shown to parents and elders — in fact all the observances customary in the group on various occasions. Regarding the instruction, properly so-called, of the children in the traditional beliefs of the group, this is the duty of clearly specified elderly persons, male or female, according as the children are boys or girls.

In many tribes there is an initiation during which the children, having reached a certain age differing from tribe to tribe, are given more intensive instruction and are subject to stricter discipline to prepare them immediately for full participation in the life of the community. This is a major event even in the life of the group as it assures to the group devoted and well-disciplined members. The traditional interest of all the adults in the up-bringing of the children of the group will prepare them to help, according to their responsibilities, in the Christian education of the children of the local Christian community. It will prepare the parents especially to shoulder their responsibilities in this matter with regard to their own children.

The traditional initiation discipline has its parallel in the Christian life in the introduction of Christian children to more responsible Christian life at the time of confirmation. They are then generally given a more thorough Christian instruction and training, and the grace of the sacrament comes to strengthen them in their following of Christ. African Christians could easily be brought to see the importance for the Christian community of this Christian rite, and as parents, to co-operate in making it as fruitful as possible for their children.

In the African family group orphaned children are cared for by the group. The sick, the aged and those who are disabled in any way, are also considered the responsibility of the group, though they are looked after more immediately by the households to which they belong. This natural human kindness, so characteristic of African tradition, is an ideal introduction to the Christian duty of helping those in need, especially among one's own relatives.

An important consequence of the brotherhood between members of the same family group, and even of the same clan, is the duty of hospitality by which each member of the group is bound to offer food and shelter to any member of his group who needs it. In fact in Buganda and the neighbouring regions it is the custom to offer hospitality even to strangers. The guest, on his part, especially if he is staying several days, renders to his host whatever service he can by his work. This openhandedness which to the African is instinctive and the most natural thing in the world is a great asset to the African Christian in practising Christian charity through sharing all he has, not only with travellers, but also with all those in want whom Providence brings in his way.

We saw that the African helps his local community with his labour in a variety of ways. For him, community service is a normal thing. He co-operates with others on occasions which call for joint effort. In particular he is accustomed to help in looking after buildings used by the community as such, and also roads, common water supplies and cattle enclosures. Of course, the kind of service expected from individuals differs from region to region according to custom and need, but the tradition of community service is very strong everywhere in Africa.

Because of this tradition the African Christian will easily understand that he must help his local Christian community to provide for its material needs — a church, a school, a house for the catechist and lodging for a visiting priest — and to help in their maintenance. He will see the service he renders as his contribution of charity to the local unit of the worldwide Christian family and its members. Moreover, his Christian outlook, which is one of service to all in charity, should prompt him to be generous in contributing to the welfare of the local community of men in the various ways which present themselves to him.

The Second Vatican Council, in its Decree on the Church's Missionary Activity (*Ad Gentes*) directed that whatever is naturally good in the racial cultures of newly evangelized peoples is to be preserved and assimilated by the Church as it develops among these peoples. 'The seed which is the Word of God sprouts from the good ground watered by divine dew. From this ground the seed draws nourishing elements which it transforms and assimilates into itself. Finally it bears much fruit. Thus, in imitation of the plan of the Incarnation, the young churches, rooted in Christ and built up on the foundation of the apostles, take to themselves in a wonderful exchange all the riches of the nations which were given to Christ as an inheritance (Ps. 2:8). From the customs and traditions of their people, from their widom and their learning, from their arts and sciences, these churches borrow all those things which can contribute to the glory of their Creator, the revelation of the Saviour's grace or the proper arrangement of Christian Life' (*Ad Gentes* 22).

After belief in a supreme being, creator of the universe, good and just, it would be difficult to find in the ancient African cultures an element more worthy of preservation and assimilation by the young African churches, or more useful to the African nations now growing towards maturity, than the African's traditional brotherliness and community involvement.

30 The Place of Women in the Christian Community
Bernadette Kunambi

Mrs. Kunambi is one of Africa's prominent Christian laywomen. As a member of the Tanzanian Parliament, leader of the Tanzanian Women's Union, head of the Tanzanian Union of Catholic Women, and not least as devoted wife and mother, she is well qualified to speak on behalf of women in Africa. Women writers and speakers are, alas, all too rare in Africa, and, although she is the only representative of her sex in this collection of writers, her views are nothing if not forthright. She has both praise and blame for the Church. On the one hand the Church has been in the forefront of promoting the dignity of women. On the other, it does not help them adequately to face the challenge of modern life — least of all, paradoxically enough, within the Church itself. In the Church women are second class citizens.

The general attitude of man to woman, not only in Africa, has made woman in many cases unable to take her rightful place as a complete human being both in the family and in society at large. She was not associated directly with decision making. She was not allowed to have a say, or even to express consent concerning the person who was to marry her. When married, she would not be considered to own her own property. Even if she was the firstborn, she would not be entitled to inherit anything from her father.

In recent times, in the wake of Western civilization brought by Western Governments and of Christianity brought by the missionaries — also from the West — there has been an evolution in the place of woman in the family as well as in society. This has brought about a feeling of emancipation for woman, the tendency towards more and more independence, both on the individual and on the family level.

This evolution, welcome as it has been, has not however been an undiluted blessing to woman. For both Christianity and Western domination, through their Western way of life, their system of education, law and administration, brought about a conflict between the old and the new; even more, it removed the African woman, and the man too, from the traditional way of life without enabling either to assimilate adequately the Western way of life, thereby creating a vacuum that is still unfilled.

While Christianity and a Western type of education gave the African woman the feeling of independence and the ability to stand on her own, to make decisions both in the family and in society, it robbed her of the traditional protection of the extended family system and of society, which in the past was the cornerstone of stability in married life. Further, it made her, as a mother, unable to have full control of her grown-up children, both boys and girls, which is the backbone of good citizenship and a proper preparation for future married life. This is the main dilemma of the African woman today: she is gaining what she wants, but she is losing what she needs.

However, it cannot be overemphasized, motherhood and the care of the home constitute woman's most essential role in the family. In my view, the women ought to satisfy herself as to her full competence in this role before involving herself in other social and civic activities. If you make your men happy at home, they will be proud of you; they will be more sociable to others, more productive in their thinking and work; they will build a sound foundation for happy and lasting marriages and united families. At the same time, if many homes are like that, we have built a sound, happy, productive society for the integral development of Africa. On the other hand, if we neglect our husbands and the home, we create dissension in our homes, and eventually disturb the equilibrium of society, be it of the Church or the nation.

This, however, should not be taken to mean support for the unwelcome attitudes of men who want to treat their wives as cattle or slaves. What I mean is that the woman, with her motherly instincts, her woman's intuition and whatever education has added to it, ought to use her discretion in doing what will make her husband and her home happy. Her influence in the home is very important.

The other equally important role of the woman is that of mother and educator of her children. We all believe that the education of children in the family is a joint responsibility of both parents. But we know, too, that anywhere in the world, and particularly in Africa, the general education of the child at home is given mainly through the mother, especially during the formative period, when the mother's influence on the child is decisive.

The role of the mother as educator is extremely important, since the way children are brought up is largely the way they will live and look at society and the world when they are grown up. The children of today are the nation of tomorrow. For a Christian mother this role is even more important as the mother has the best opportunity to instil into the child all the good concepts of Christianity at this early and most important stage of character formation.

The mother has an even more special responsibility in relation to the character formation of her daughters and their friends. For the mother knows well what a girl should expect and can prepare her for all eventualities, including step-by-step preparation for marriage.

In Africa the woman, as a human being, like the man, is often puzzled, and even confused, by Christianity as presented to her. What is puzzling is not the Bible as a whole, for most of what is in the Bible is very close to the traditional way of life in Africa even today. It is not even the Gospel, for the message of Our Lord is simple and straightforward: it is love and all that constitutes charity. The problem to the woman, as to the man, is the set-up of the Church as brought to Africa.

The African woman, as a woman, and perhaps any woman anywhere, faces what may be the greatest challenge in the Church. It is the problem of finding herself at a loss to know what the place of the woman is in the Church. The Church teaches equality of all men (which includes women) before God, and yet the woman often finds herself a second, if not a third, class citizen in the Church.

Africa's development asks for woman's integral development. The only extra thing here is a plea, this time to the hierarchy of the Church, that the Biblical and Church teaching that all men (including women) are equal should not only appear in writing, or be heard from pulpits, but should be put into practice. By this I mean that woman should be fully integrated and involved in every aspect of life. For any-body to be fully effective in any organization or structure, the first and foremost condition is that the person must be appreciated as a human being and accepted as equal. Women can be a great and effective force in the growth of the Church, if properly mobilized. It is essential that they have their rightful place in all Church structures.

In conclusion, therefore, the women of Africa can contri-bute considerably to the development of Africa and the Church, and to my knowledge quite a few have already done so and are still doing so. What all women need are: opportu-nity, facilities, encouragement, awakening and acceptance in their rightful place in society. Give women the tools and, with God's blessing, they will complete the job. And you women, for the sake of Africa, life up to your responsi-bilities!

31 Kimbu Village Prayer
Aylward Shorter

*This prayer-poem was composed by the editor of this
volume as a kind of finale. It is addressed to the Spirit of
God, stirring in Africa, and it attempts to take up a number
of themes that have emerged from the contributions of the
writers represented in this book. From 1964 to 1970 Aylward
Shorter carried out fieldwork in Ukimbu, an area of south-
western Tanzania, spending nearly two years living
continuously in a Kimbu village. The Kimbu cultivate
palisaded clearings in a vast and dense woodland,
dominated by numerous rock-crowned hills. The scene is set
as the village wakes to a new day, and continues with the
communal activities of the villagers, millet-threshing,
house-building, honey-gathering (often following the
honey-bird or honey-guide), hunting, fishing and wedding
rituals. For the Christian, co-operative living reveals the
presence of Christ, and points to the final reconciliation of
humankind in God.*

Island hill-tops
Pierce the broads of mist
That roof the matutinal trees,
And smooth-flanked boulders
Nestle in the shock of green,
Like conus-emblems
In a chieftain's plaited hair.
Your Spirit,
Early-stirring in the morning atmosphere,
Accompanies the bell-birds'
Momently duet,
Reiterates
The red-breast cuckoo's monody.
Your herds glide silently
Among arboreal spears,
Obedient
To the beckoning Master of the wild;
And, with the honey-guide,
You chatter overhead

To plot
The complex flight-plan of the homing bees.
Within the palisaded clearing breathes
The rustling maize.
A dog is barking,
And the monitory cock
Awakes the sleeping village
From his makeshift minaret.
The blue-grey smoke-wisps curl
From every mushroom-thatch;
And soon the wattle doors
Are set aside,
And blanket-swaddled denizens emerge
To prod the dying embers
And to down
The early-morning can of gruel.
While in the compound
Watchful ancestors sleep on,
Their earthen coverlets
Pegged down with corner-sticks.
Yours is the thread of life that binds
The living and the dead,
And yours
The quick of our relatedness.
Among the millet-threshers
And the men that build
A neighbour's homestead,
Or the forest slash
To let the sun's rays sweeten
A new farm
Among the shouting fisher-folk
That splash
And scare the mudfish
From the shallow river bottoms,
For huntsmen, yes,
And honey-gatherers,
You are the bond.
You are the cloth that binds
The bobbing babies to the backs
Of mothers
In their rhythmic pounding

Of the grain,
The single calico that hides
The sponsor and the tearful bride
At village nuptials,
You, the milk-white paste
With which the earnest wedding-guests
Anoint the unassuming pair.

These, the faces
Of the Universal Brother,
Earthbound kindred's loving
Lineage-head,
Defender
Of diminished humankind.
You spark in us
The glint of recognition and
The present hope
Of sharing in divine community.
God's programme for
World-villagization.

Aylward Shorter
Tanzania, September 1977

References to Part Two

The numbers are those given to the texts produced in this anthology.

1. Camara Laye, 'The Soul of Africa in Guinea', in *African Writers on African Writing*, ed. G.D. Killam (London, Heinemann Educational Books, 1973), pp. 158-62; used by permission of the author.

2. Michel Kayoya, *My Father's Footprints*, trans. Aylward Shorter and Marie-Agnes Baldwin (Nairobi, East African Publishing House, 1973), pp. 89-91; © translation Aylward Shorter.

3. Kenneth Kaunda, *Letter to My Children* (Worcester and London, Ebenezer Baylis and Son Ltd., 1973), pp. 17-23; used by permission of the publishers.

4. Extracts from an unpublished translation by Aylward Shorter and Wandera-Chagenda of Michel Kayoya's *Entre Deux Mondes* (Bujumbura, 1970); © translation Aylward Shorter.

5. Leopold Sédar Senghor, *On African Socialism* (London, Pall Mall Press Ltd., 1961), p. 141 and pp. 144-48; used by permission of the publishers.

6. Poem by Wandera-Chagenda, published under the title 'Massai-Warrior-Fashion' in *Sharing* (Gaba Publications) 7, no.4 (September 1975):5; © Wandera-Chagenda, reprinted by permission of the author.

7. Camara Laye, *The Radiance of the King* (London, Collins Fontana Books, 1965), pp. 280-84; used by permission of the publishers.

8. Harry Sawyerr, *Creative Evangelism* (London, Lutterworth

Press, 1968), pp.72-74: used by permission of the publishers.

9. Chukwundum B. Okolo, 'Diminished Man and Theology: A Third World Perspective', *African Ecclesiastical Review* (hereafter referred to as AFER), 18, no.2 (1976): 83-86; reprinted by permission of the editor.

10. Fritz Pawelzik, *I Lie on My Mat and Pray* (New York, Friendship Press, 1964,) pp. 42-43; used by permission of the publishers.

11. Lawrenti Magesa, 'Return to the World — Towards a Theocentric Existentialism in Africa', *AFER* 16, no. 3 (1974): 278-80; reprinted by permission of the editor.

12. Archbishop J. B. Zoa, 'Committed Christians Building a New Africa', *AFER* 8, no. 2 (1966): 99-104; reprinted by permission of the editor.

13. Unpublished poem by Wandera-Chagenda, manuscript in the possession of the editor; © Wandera-Chagenda, printed by permission of the author.

14. Julius K. Nyerere, *Freedom and Development* (Oxford, Oxford University Press, 1973), pp. 215-16, 219-22, 223-24, 225-26 and 227. (Extracts from an address made in 1970 to the Maryknoll Congress); © Julius K. Nyerere, used by permission of the author.

15. Michael Kayoya, *My Father's Footprints*, pp.125-28.

16. Bishop Henry Okullu, 'Comment on Tribal Hatred', *AFER* 14, no. 4 (1972): 341-42; reprinted by permission of the editor.

17. Poem by Wandera-Chagenda, first published under this title in *Sharing* (Gaba Publications) 7, no. 4 (September 1975): 5; © Wandera-Chagenda, reprinted by permission of the author.

18. J. Akin Omoyajowo, 'Christianity as a Unifying Factor in a Developing Country', *AFER* 17, no.2 (1975): 74-79; reprinted by permission of the editor.

19. Dominic Mwasaru, 'The Challenge of Africanizing the Church', *AFER* 16, no.3 (1974): 291-93; reprinted by permission of the editor.

20. Charles Nyamiti, *The Scope of African Theology* (Eldoret, Gaba Publications, 1973), p.6; reprinted by permission of the Director of Gaba Publications.

21. Poem by Wandera-Chagenda, unpublished manuscript in the possession of the editor; © Wandera-Chagenda, printed by permission of the author.

22. Laurenti Magesa, 'Catholic Yet African', *AFER* 15, no.2 (1973): 110-11: reprinted by permission of the editor.

23. Raymond Arazu, 'Towards Contemplative Prayer', *AFER* 14, no.2 (1972): 135-39; reprinted by permission of the editor.

24. Kenneth Kaunda, *op. cit.*, pp. 57-58 and 103-7; used by permission of the publishers.

25. Christopher Mwoleka, 'Trinity and Community', *AFER* 17, no.4 (1975): 203-26; reprinted by permission of the editor.

26. Camillus Lyimo, 'The Quest for a Relevant African Theology', *AFER* 18, no.3 (1976): 140-43; reprinted by permission of the editor.

27. Harry Sawyerr, *op. cit.*, pp. 93-96 and 111-12; used by permission of the publishers.

28. Kenneth Kaunda, *A Humanist in Africa* (London, Longman Green and Co. Ltd., 1966), pp. 22-28; used by permission of the publishers.

29. Damian Lwasa, 'African Traditional Community as a Preparation for Christian Community Life', *Omnis Terra* (Sacred Congregation for Evangelizing Peoples, Rome) 45, no.4 (May 1972): 359-65; reprinted by permission of the editor.

30. Mrs B.N. Kunambi, 'Women of Africa: Awake!', *AFER* 13, no.4 (1971): 302-4; reprinted by permission of the editor.

31. Unpublished poem by the editor; © Aylward Shorter.